After school, Wendell brought Judith Hender-son to meet the horses.

"You're going to love them!"

She was very polite, saying "hello" and petting each of them on the nose. She had even brought her own sugar cubes and gave one to each of them. Wendell was right. Judith did like the horses. And the horses liked Judith. Each of them told Wendell so.

"Did you hear that, Judith?"

But try as she might, Judith couldn't hear the horses speak. So she just stood and watched.

"Don't worry, Judith, you'll hear them. It just takes practice," Wendell said.

THE HORSES OF CENTRAL PARK

Michael Slade

AN
APPLE
PAPERBACK

SCHOLASTIC INC.
New York Toronto London Auckland Sydney

ISBN 0-590-44068-3

12 11 10 9 8 7 6 5 4 3 2 1   3   4 5 6 7 8 9/9

Printed in the U.S.A.

40

*For C.S.K. who talks
to the horses.*
                    —M.S.

THE HORSES OF CENTRAL PARK

ONE

Wendell Riley Randolph turned twelve on April twelfth, which made him very happy. It was going to be a special year. Only once in your whole life are your birthday and age the same number and this was that once in Wendell's life. Yes, this year was definitely going to be special.

On the morning of April twelfth, Wendell stood looking at himself in the mirror. He was wearing the new pair of glasses he had gotten, sort of a birthday present but not really. As he had explained to his parents, "Even though I need a new pair of glasses and even though I want a new pair of frames, glasses aren't exactly the sort of thing you give someone as a birthday present. Birthday presents are supposed to be special. Glasses are just something you get 'cause you need them!"

All the same, Wendell was glad he had gotten them. They were the sort of glasses a rock star might wear. Wendell looked in the mirror and strummed an imaginary guitar. Then, as he looked at his reflection, he brushed his hair out of his eyes and remembered what his grandmother Randolph was always saying. "Wendell, you have the most beautiful hair. It's not blond. It's gold."

Now as Wendell looked in the mirror, he remembered that old people were often making comments about his hair or his freckles — "just a few, not a whole faceful, just the right amount" — or about how handsome he was going to be when he grew up, and how popular. Wendell looked and looked, but he never quite saw it. He only saw Wendell Riley Randolph, who was okay-looking and all, in an average-sort-of-way, not ugly or anything, but not what he would call handsome, either.

He looked in the mirror that morning of April twelfth and said to himself, "Well, Wendell, you look about the same to me. Nothing's changed that I can see. All that's happened is you've grown another year older."

Ever since he could remember, Wendell had always looked forward to growing a year older. Because it meant he was getting closer to growing into his name. Wendell hated his name. Wendell Riley Randolph. It sounded so . . . *old*. There was another boy in school who hated his name, Leslie Scott Samuelson. Leslie just used his middle name, Scott. But Riley was no better than Wendell. If it had been his father's name, Wendell could have been called Junior, but his father's name was John. And there was no good way to shorten Wendell Riley Randolph. Sometimes, when some of the kids at school teased him, they called him Wendy. That was the worst. Wendy Riley Randolph!!!! Those were the days when, during dinner, he would tell his parents that he hated them for giving him such a terrible name.

"And just as soon as I'm old enough, I'm going to go to court and change it!"

And his father would say he understood but that: "When you're older and you've become a lawyer or a doctor or a professor, you'll be glad you have such an important-sounding name, and not just a plain, ordinary one like John."

And his mother would remind him of a certain cowboy shirt that Wendell's Uncle Chip had sent him some time ago. It was much too big and Wendell couldn't wear it, so he hated it. Recently, however, he had grown into the shirt and his mother had to fight to get him to take it off long enough for it to be washed.

"The same will be true with your name. And,"

she added, "I'll bet that pretty soon the girls will start thinking that Wendell is a very interesting name indeed. And start wanting to get to know this Wendell Riley Randolph a little better."

That's when Wendell would remember Judith (never-call-me-Judy) Henderson. Judith was Wendell's best friend and confidante. They had met in the fourth grade, in Miss Lieb's class. Even then, Judith had had her own particular style. Her long, brown hair was always pulled back into not-quite-a-ponytail and she wore funny vests and lots of different patterns all sort of thrown together. And even then, Judith didn't care what anybody else thought. Wendell liked that. He liked it a lot. Judith wasn't exactly fat. But she wasn't exactly skinny, either. "It's just baby fat," she would say. "The same kind as Marilyn Monroe had. If you want to grow up to be gorgeous, you have to give nature a little something to work with!"

Wendell couldn't remember exactly how or why he and Judith had become friends. Maybe because they both got teased. Maybe because they were both only children. Maybe not.

And lately, Judith (never-call-me-Judy) Henderson had taken to mentioning almost every day that Wendell was "such a distinguished name. The kind of name a girl enjoys saying . . . a lot!"

Wendell and his parents lived on the tenth

floor of an apartment building in New York City and he went to the Filmore School. What Wendell did in school was not particularly different from what any other twelve year old did. He studied English and math and history and science and art and music and gym. And sometimes he did well and sometimes he did less well. And sometimes he was attentive and sometimes, but not very often, he got into trouble.

But what Wendell did after school was special. Every day after school, Wendell did something that no one else in his class did. Something that no one else in his whole school did. Every afternoon Wendell walked to Central Park South, across from the Plaza Hotel, where the horse-drawn carriages called hansom cabs waited for fares, and Wendell talked to the horses. Yes, Wendell Riley Randolph talked to the horses. And he didn't just pat them on the nose and say hello. Wendell really talked to them. And the horses answered. They had very interesting conversations.

Wendell learned how to talk with horses from his uncle Chip (the same one who'd sent him the cowboy shirt). Chip was Wendell's mother's younger brother. He lived on a horse farm in New Jersey and last summer he had invited Wendell to visit for two weeks all by himself. They were two of the best weeks of Wendell's life. Uncle Chip taught Wendell all about horses. How to feed them. How to brush them. How to ride them. And how to talk to them.

"Talk to horses?" Wendell had asked.

"Well, certainly," said Uncle Chip, "and more importantly, how to listen to their answers."

"Listen to their answers?! Horses can't talk, Uncle Chip!"

"Oh, yes, they can. Maybe not like you and me, but they're very intelligent and they certainly can talk."

"I don't believe you."

"Well, yesterday you wouldn't have believed that horses had a sense of humor and could play jokes on people, but thanks to Simon you believe that now."

He had a point there. Just yesterday Wendell had seen how funny a horse can be. Uncle Chip and some of his friends had been standing in the yard talking. Wendell was there, too, but he wasn't very much interested in investments and taxes, so he was the only one who noticed that Simon, Uncle Chip's favorite horse, was wandering closer and closer until he was just a few steps away from them. Uncle Chip and Pete and Will and Marty kept talking. Suddenly, Simon leaned all the way forward, opened his mouth, and ever so gingerly took the collar of Marty's shirt in his teeth, tugged a little, then let go, stepped back, and looked off in another direction.

"Who did that?" asked Marty.

"Who did what?" answered Pete.

"Who pulled on my shirt?"

"No one pulled on your shirt. We're all standing here talking."

Wendell just stared at Simon. A few moments later, when the conversation had resumed, Simon looked at Wendell, winked, stepped forward, leaned in, tugged on Marty's shirt, then stepped back to where he had been. And by the time Marty had turned around, Simon was looking up at a passing cloud that was sort of shaped like a giant duck.

"*Who did that!*?" yelled Marty.

"Who did what?" Pete answered, sounding a little annoyed.

"Okay, guys!" Marty said, turning away from Chip, Pete, and Will. "Hey, Wendell, did you see who pulled my shirt?"

"No, Marty, I didn't." Wendell turned around, held his stomach, and pinched his arms to keep from laughing out loud.

"Marty, are we talking or are we playi games?" This time it was Uncle Chip asking.

"I'm talking," answered Marty, "but som body here is playing games."

"Marty!" cried Will, who was getting perated.

Wendell, still holding his stomach and pinching his arms, was doing all right. He was shaking a little, but he wasn't laughing, when suddenly he noticed that Marty had turned around again and Simon was tugging his collar a third time.

"Who did that!?" Marty sounded very angry.

"Marty!" yelled Will.

"Enough is enough!" Marty's face had gotten very red.

Wendell couldn't hold it in any longer. The laughter exploded out of him as he shrieked, "It's Simon! It's Simon! It's the horse! It's Simon the horse!"

"What?" said Marty.

Simon was swatting a fly.

"It's Simon!" Wendell said, still laughing. "He keeps sneaking up and pulling your collar with his teeth!"

So, remembering the joke Simon had played on Marty, Wendell was at least willing to consider the possibility that horses could talk. Uncle Chip taught Wendell all about talking with horses. How to look deep into their big eyes, all the way into their souls, ". . . because the eyes are the mirrors of the soul." And how to listen, not just with your ears, but with your eyes and with your heart. "It isn't easy. It takes practice."

t then, the day before Wendell was set to e he came running from the corral to the house, calling out, "Uncle Chip! Uncle Chip! I heard him! I heard him! He talked! Simon talked and I heard him! He told me he knew this was my last day and that he was going to miss me and hoped I'd come back soon. And he said, wasn't that a good joke he played on Marty! Uncle Chip! He talked to me! At first I thought I was imagining it, but I wasn't. He talked to me! He talked to me and I heard him!"

When he returned home, Wendell decided to keep in practice.

But how? Wendell lived in New York City. Now, New York City is good for doing lots of things — things like seeing the dinosaurs at the Museum of Natural History whenever you want, or the Egyptian mummies at the Metropolitan Museum of Art, or even watching them blow up the giant balloons for the Thanksgiving Day parade. And though New York City is a great place to find rock stars and movie stars walking down the street, New York City is not exactly the place you'd think of to find horses. Unless, like Wendell, you lived fairly close to Central Park and, like Wendell, you stopped to remember all the horse-drawn carriages that lined up on Central Park South (which wasn't very far from Wendell's school) to give people rides.

And so every day after school, Wendell talked to the horses that pulled the hansom cabs through Central Park. He learned a lot from those horses. He learned that sometimes they like to talk and sometimes they don't, just like people. And that they definitely don't like to talk while they're eating.

This went on for many months, and in all that time Wendell never told anyone. It was his secret. He didn't tell the kids at school because he knew they would make fun of him.

"Wendy Riley Randolph talks to horses!"

And he didn't tell his parents because he knew they would tell him to start spending less time alone and more time making friends. Wendell Riley Randolph didn't understand why it was, but it seemed that all his life, whenever he was happily drawing or reading or playing pretend games, his parents would tell him to go find some friends to play with.

Sometimes parents were awfully hard to understand. So Wendell didn't tell anyone how he spent his afternoons. Not even Judith (never-call-me-Judy) Henderson.

TWO

April twenty-first was a glorious day. There was no chill in the air, no cloud in the sky, and the tulips in Central Park had decided to poke their heads up and say hello to the world. The first real day of spring was not a time to be stuck in school.

Wendell liked school enough. Filmore was a likeable school. "It's a small, private school, founded in 1865, and all sorts of important people have attended it," Wendell had told Uncle Chip's friends. "It's on the West Side of Manhattan, almost directly across the park from my apartment building."

When Wendell started at Filmore as a kinder-gartner, his father would drop him off before going downtown to work in the morning. And in the afternoon, his mother would pick him up. It was the same way in first grade (although sometimes one of his friend's parents would pick up a group of them). But when Wendell started third grade, his parents agreed that he was old enough to take the bus across town by himself. And in fifth grade, they started letting him ride his bicycle.

Filmore has a high school just a few doors down the street from the lower school and, though many kids transfer to different high schools when they reach the ninth grade, Wendell planned on staying at Filmore all the way. "I mean, it's our school," he had told Judith, who was in complete agreement.

So, Wendell's not wanting to be in school wasn't anything against Filmore. It was just that the first real day of spring was not a time to be stuck in ANY school.

For Wendell Riley Randolph and the rest of the kids, the hours had never passed so slowly. Was this really just *one* day?! Had he somehow fallen into a time warp where it was always going to be a quarter to three?! Was it still going to be sunny and warm when they got out or would Mother Nature play a prank on them and turn it all cold, gray, and wet?!

RRRRRRRRIIIIIIIIIIIINNNNNNNGGGGGG!!!!!

Five hundred boys and girls came bounding and galloping out the doors of the Filmore School.

"Who's coming to the park to play soccer?"

"I am."

"Me, too."

"Oh, Wendy! Do you want to play soccer?"

"We'll give you a free kick."

"Yeah, right in your butt."

"Ow!" cried Wendell as one of the boys kicked him.

"Wendell?"

"Yes, Judith?"

"Don't mind them."

"Hey, Wendy, are you gonna come?"

"He's too busy with Judy Henderson."

"Betcha he's gonna take her to the Dance-A-Thon."

"Ha, ha, ha, ha, ha, ha, ha, ha, ha."

"They're just jealous, Wendell. Do you want to go for a walk? We could go to the carousel in Central Park. That's one of my favorite things to do. I always pretend that the painted ponies are real horses, only the music casts a spell on them and keeps them stuck on the carousel. But at night, when the music has stopped and the people are gone, they wake up and run free all through the park until morning."

Wendell was wishing Judith wouldn't talk so much.

"That's silly, isn't it?"

"No, Judith, it's not silly," Wendell shifted his feet impatiently.

"Do you want to come?"

"Gee, Judith, I can't today. I've got something important to do." Wendell was thinking about the real horses and wondering what they thought of this beautiful day. "Maybe another time."

"Like tomorrow?"

"Yeah, maybe tomorrow. I've got to go."

"I'll call you later. Sometimes, Wendell Riley Randolph, you are awfully strange."

But Wendell Riley Randolph hadn't heard her because he had gone racing off toward Central Park South.

The men and women who drive the hansom cabs had taken special care to wash and polish the carriages so that they sparkled and shone in the bright sunlight. Wendell had seen all of these carriages many times before. He had seen them practically every day for months and months and months. But now it was as if he was seeing them for the first time. How beautiful they were — each in its own particular way. There was an elegant black carriage, all enclosed (like a car), with little windowpanes and doors for getting in and out of it. It had brass lamps on all four corners, which had been polished until they glistened. There was a white carriage with a green-and-white striped canopy top, which was adorned all over with fresh carnations. There were many open carriages, some black, some white, some red, and one that was painted the brightest of yellows. The yellow carriage had a bouquet of tulips painted on either side, and in the front, by the driver's seat, was a bucket filled with fresh tulips.

As different as the carriages were, so were the drivers. There was a young woman dressed in a tuxedo and top hat. There was an old man, in an even older suit of evening clothes, with the unlit stub of a cigar in his mouth. There was one young man in jeans with a white shirt and tie, and another young man in a sports jacket with patches on the elbows and a daisy in his lapel.

Wendell made his way down the line of standing horses. He spoke to each of them in turn and found that in place of the usual depression about being overworked and tired, every one of the horses was as excited as a foal about spring's awakening. Even Old Barnaby, who never spoke but just stared blankly at the ground. Old Barnaby, whose driver mistakenly called him Paco, and whose eyes were always dead and clouded over. Old Barnaby, who, (the other horses had told Wendell), used to be in show business and who had, in between stories about filming movies and television shows and commercials, tried to convince them to stand up for their rights and put an end to their terrible working conditions. Old Barnaby, who, the other horses confided to Wendell, was now kept on drugs so that he couldn't make any more trouble. Even Old Barnaby seemed to perk up when Wendell said, "Isn't this a glorious day!" And just for a moment, Wendell thought he saw the clouds clear from Old Barnaby's eyes and a flash of something that seemed to say, "I'm still here," before the drugs took control again. Wendell patted Old Barnaby on the nose, slipped him a sugar cube, and moved on to Elmer.

Elmer was Wendell's favorite Central Park horse. Partly because he was the first one who spoke to Wendell, partly because they both hated their names, and mostly because they just liked each other.

"How's it going, Elmer?"

"Not too bad."

Elmer had spent most of his life in and around Central Park. He had been born on a little farm in the country, but they hadn't needed another horse so Elmer was sold to a man who gave pony rides to children in the park. Then, when he grew too big for that, he was sold to the riding stables in the park where adults took him out for runs on the trails. That was fun. And he got to know every inch of Central Park. But then he got too old and the stables sold him to the hansom cab company. That was several years ago. Elmer missed running in the park.

"It's kind of nice, today," Elmer continued, "having the warm sun on my face."

"I'm sure it is."

"And the people are all friendlier."

"That's true."

"And the drivers take extra care to polish the carriages and brush us down."

"You look years younger."

"Why, thank you, Wendell. When you have a little attention paid to you and people seem to care, why it makes a horse feel — "

Suddenly Elmer stopped speaking. He had seen something on the street. Something very upsetting. He turned away, looked at the ground, and was silent.

"What is it, Elmer? What's wrong?"

Wendell looked at the street and understood. There, trotting down Central Park South, was one of New York City's mounted policemen, all dressed up in his fancy uniform, and under him was the snootiest, most conceited horse Wendell had ever seen. The horse was beautiful, there was no mistaking that, and perfectly groomed — his coat and saddle gleamed in the sunlight. He seemed to have stepped out of a picture book or one of the horse shows Wendell had seen advertised. As he proudly headed east

with his tail held high in the air and his nose
stuck up even further, he didn't even glance at
the hansom cab horses, and yet he seemed to
say, "Look at me! I'm one of New York's finest.
You call yourselves horses? Compare your life
to mine. I go wherever I want, all over the city.
You're just old slaves. Look at you! Why, you're
not even good enough for the glue factory!"

Wendell Riley Randolph turned back to his
friends in time to see them all, one by one, turn
their heads away from the police horse and
stare at the ground or off into nothing. All the
excitement, spirit, and joy disappeared from
their faces. They suddenly looked old. Very old.
And tired. Very tired. And worn out. Very worn
out.

"Hey, Elmer, that sun is getting awfully warm!"
said Wendell, trying to restart a conversation.

Elmer didn't answer.

"Don't worry about that stuck-up police
horse. You're as good as he is. Why, you're
better than he is."

But Elmer didn't even look up. And neither
did Winston or Molly or Archibald or Quentin
or Angelina or Samantha or Cromwell or Chloe or
Old Barnaby. Finally, Wendell gave up. "Good-
bye," he said. "See you later." But no one
answered. He turned and started toward home.
He no longer noticed the beautiful blue sky or
the warm sun or the tulips beginning to bloom.

Everything looked cold and gray to Wendell.
And Wendell Riley Randolph looked cold and
gray as well. He looked just as depressed as
Elmer and the other horses.

"There must be something I can do to help
those horses feel better about themselves. But
what?"

Wendell didn't remember anything about his
walk home. He must have walked east on Fifty-
ninth Street until he got to Lexington Avenue.
And he must have turned left on Lexington
Avenue and walked up to Seventy-seventh
Street. And he must have turned right on Seventy-seventh Street until he got to number 107.
And he must have walked into the building, past
the doorman, and into the elevator. And he
must have said hi to his mother. And he must
have gone into his room. But Wendell didn't
remember. All he could remember was what
happened when Elmer and the other horses saw
that police horse. Maybe he didn't walk home
at all. Maybe he took a bus.

THREE

The next morning, Wendell didn't feel very much like going to school.

"But I feel sick, Mom. Honest."

"There is nothing wrong with you, Wendell," his mother replied. "Other than the fact that you've been moping around the apartment ever since you came home from school yesterday. I don't think you said ten words all last night. And you barely touched your dinner. Now, what's going on?"

Wendell wanted to tell her about the horses. He did. He wanted to tell her about what had happened with that snooty police horse. He wanted to tell her exactly what was bothering him. He really did. But when he opened his mouth, all that came out was, "Nothing."

"Wendell" — his mother was not about to let up — "are you having some sort of trouble at school?"

"No." Wendell wished he had never said anything about staying home. What had he been thinking? Because if she let him skip school, then she certainly wouldn't let him go off to the park later. And that's what he really wanted to do. He wanted to go and talk to the horses.

"This isn't a repeat of what happened a couple of years ago, is it, Wendell? You know what I'm talking about. Is there something I should know?"

Wendell knew exactly what his mother was talking about. Back when he was nine, a group of older boys had taken to teasing Wendell at school. It had gotten so bad that Wendell started pretending he was sick so he could stay home and avoid them. But that was a long time ago. Why did mothers have to remember everything?

"No, Mom. Everything's fine."

"Wendell!" His mother was not convinced.

Okay, thought Wendell, here goes. "You see, Mom," he said, "I got into trouble in school yesterday." His mother gave him a look. "Not big trouble," Wendell continued.

"Oh?" said his mother.

"I mean not trouble like I did something

bad." Wendell was stalling, trying to think of something to tell his mother to get himself out of this jam.

"What sort of trouble?" His mother had gotten very quiet, which was never a good sign.

And then it came to Wendell. "You see, we're studying debating in school and yesterday we drew lots to see who would debate against whom today and I picked Andy McDonald, who's only the best debater in the whole school." Wendell saw his mother's face relax. "And we're going to be graded based on how well we do," Wendell continued, "which means I'm going to get a terrible grade because I'm never going to win against Andy McDonald. And that's why I didn't want to go to school, because if I'm not there today, Andy will get paired off with somebody else and then tomorrow I'll get paired off with somebody else." It wasn't completely a lie. They *were* studying debating. And Wendell *had* gotten paired off with Andy. But the debate wasn't until next week. And Andy McDonald was probably the worst debater in the class.

"Wendell" — now his mother was smiling — "I'm sure you'll do just fine." And, as she gave him a kiss, she added, "Now, hurry up or you're going to be late."

Wendell paid very little attention in school. In fact, it was only after he was told that if he didn't straighten up he was going to have to stay after school for detention that he began to concentrate at all. But even then, Wendell kept thinking about the horses.

When at last it was three o'clock and school was over, Wendell almost knocked four different students down as he raced out of the building. One of them was Judith. "Wendell!" she fairly shouted.

"I can't talk now. I'm in a hurry," Wendell answered.

"We were supposed to go to the carousel today! Don't you remember?" Judith called after him. But Wendell couldn't hear her. He was already halfway down the street.

"Don't worry about it, Wendell," Elmer responded after Wendell told him how upset he still was. "I've gotten over it. We've all gotten over it. It's just one of those things. We, or at least I, shouldn't have let it bother me so much yesterday. That was wrong."

"But, Elmer — " Wendell began.

"True," Elmer continued, "we may not have the best lot in life. But we're here, we've got each other, most of the drivers are nice enough. And we've got you — that makes up for a lot."

"Thank you," said Wendell as he scratched the tuft of golden hair that always hung down over Elmer's eyes.

"So you just put all of that nonsense that happened yesterday right out of your mind. Why, look at Cromwell up there. Do you think he's given it a second thought?"

Wendell turned to see that Cromwell, a big, muscular, dark brown horse had stepped up onto the curb with his two front legs and was actually turning his whole carriage around as he strained to see Wendell. His driver, the old man who wore evening clothes and always had a cigar in his mouth, was trying, vainly, to turn Cromwell back around.

"Whoa, Cromwell! Whoa!" cried the driver. "You've got to get down off the curb and back on the street, where you belong. Come on, Cromwell!" But because the driver never took the big, fat, cigar butt out of his mouth, it sounded more like, "Ohhh, Rommell! Ohhhh! Yahgahtahgehdow awfuh curr an bagona stree where yuh blawn. Um on Rommell!"

"You'd better go talk to him, Wendell," Elmer said, laughing, "before he gets himself into a whole mess of trouble."

"Okay," Wendell replied, "but I'll talk to you again before I go home."

"I wouldn't have it any other way," said Elmer.

He's a great horse, thought Wendell as he looked back at Elmer. It was a sort of cloudy day, but just then, a break had appeared, sending a shaft of sunlight directly onto Elmer.

It was like a giant spotlight had focused on him, attracted by Elmer's golden tan color.

"You'd better watch out, son," Cromwell's driver was saying. (He took the cigar out of his mouth when he talked to humans.) "He's being pretty ornery today." The driver had finally gotten Cromwell down off the curb and back on the street. Though if the truth be told, it was Cromwell who decided to go back to the street when he saw that Wendell was on his way.

"I'll be careful," said Wendell as he scratched Cromwell's nose.

The driver just shook his head and started walking back to one of the benches that lined the park.

"Well, it's about time you came over here!" sputtered Cromwell. "I was beginning to think that I was going to have to drag this whole carriage up onto the sidewalk, walk down there, and toss you into it to get your attention."

"I'm sorry," said Wendell quietly. "I was talking to Elmer."

"I know that," said Cromwell. "Why do you think I was trying to get your attention so badly?"

"I don't know," answered Wendell.

"Because there's something you need to know about Elmer," snorted Cromwell.

"He's not sick or anything, is he?" Wendell's heart started racing.

"No," said Cromwell, reassuringly. "At least not the way you mean."

"Well then, what is it?" Wendell realized that he had snapped at Cromwell and suddenly felt embarrassed. "I'm sorry, Cromwell. It's just that I've been so upset about what happened yesterday. And then Elmer tells me it was nothing, but I know it wasn't, and then you tell me there's something wrong with him and . . . I didn't mean to snap at you."

"Oh, fiddle-faddle!" Cromwell sputtered. "I'm not so thin-skinned as to be offended by a little thing like being snapped at." (Though secretly he was awfully pleased that Wendell was so concerned.) "But I'm glad you brought up what happened yesterday, because that's what we've got to talk about."

"Elmer told me — " Wendell began, but that was all he got out before Cromwell burst in.

"I know what Elmer told you! And it's not true! Elmer was humiliated yesterday. As were we all. But Elmer's taken it extremely badly. He wouldn't talk to any of us the rest of the day. And last night . . . I shouldn't be telling you this, but I figure if there's anyone who can help, it's you. Last night, when he thought everyone was asleep, I heard Elmer crying."

Cromwell paused a moment and then very quietly added, "I've known Elmer for over seven years and I've never . . ." His voice trailed off.

"It's not a pretty sound, when a horse cries."

All of Wendell's worst feelings returned. He felt awful.

"And, now, please don't take this the wrong way," Cromwell continued, "but I think what made it even worse for Elmer was that you were here to see the humiliation." He paused for a moment and then added, "I know it made it worse for me."

Wendell started to turn back toward Elmer.

"Don't look at him!" snorted Cromwell. "He'll know we're talking about him!"

"Oh, of course," said Wendell, feeling a little embarrassed. "But what can we do?" Wendell felt thoroughly helpless. "We need to do something. Not just for Elmer, but for all of you. We need some sort of a plan."

"As you know," Cromwell began, "I come from an old army family."

Wendell couldn't help but smile. He had heard time and again about Cromwell's army background. He had also heard, from Elmer and Molly and some of the other horses, however, that Cromwell had never really served in the army. That the army had been phasing out horses and so, as a colt, Cromwell had been sold to the carriage company. But Wendell would never bring that up to Cromwell. To do so would not only be rude, but also unnecessarily hurtful. So whenever Cromwell would go on

about army life, Wendell would just nod and
smile and listen respectfully.

"So, as I was saying," Cromwell was coming
to the end of his army story, "though I excel at
following orders, I'm not very good at coming
up with plans. For a plan, I suggest you talk to
Samantha. She was in the circus, you know. I'll
bet she knows something about plans."

Wendell thanked Cromwell, gave him one last
scratch behind the ears, then turned to the
driver and said, "See, he's okay. He just wanted
a little extra attention." The driver, who by now
was sitting on a bench reading a newspaper,
just grunted.

Cromwell was right. Samantha had been with
the circus. "I used to wear the most beautiful
headdress," she told Wendell. "Bright, bright,
red feathers, which stood out so beautifully
against my black and white spots. But," she
sighed, "my trainer made the plans. I just did
the tricks. Besides, if I knew anything about
making plans, do you think I would have let
myself wind up here when my little circus closed?
Here, where we get humiliated by civil servants!
That's all those police horses are, you know, for
all their fancy airs. Civil servants!"

Next, Wendell talked to Chloe, who was fat
and gray and always sweet. But when he asked
her if she knew anything about making plans,
she just giggled and said, "Oh, dear, me, no."

Winston was still too upset about the police horse to talk at all, so Wendell just scratched him on the big, white splotch on the left side of his otherwise all-brown neck — which Winston had made a point of telling Wendell, many months ago, was his favorite spot to be scratched.

Angelina and Quentin and Archibald were all off giving rides to groups of tourists. "Angelina and Quentin got some lovely people," Molly was telling Wendell. "But Archibald got a carriageful of the stupidest humans you'd ever want to meet." Wendell liked Molly a lot. She reminded him of his Grandmother Randolph, who always had something to say about somebody, and rarely was it particularly nice. "To begin with, two of them didn't realize they were going to have to pay for the ride. Can you believe it? They thought we were all out here just doing this for our health. Us and the drivers! I mean, there's a sign right on every carriage telling the prices! And then, the other couple . . . oh!" Molly stopped herself. "But you wanted to know about plans. The only one who's very good at making plans is Elmer. Barnaby used to be, but not since . . ." Molly just shook her head. "And don't let that Cromwell try to tell you he knows anything about plans. You know," she said, very confidentially, "he never really served in the army at all."

Wendell thanked Molly for her help, patted
her nose, and went back to say good-bye to
Elmer.

"It's getting kind of late, I've got to be going
home. I'll see you tomorrow. Okay?"

"Okay," said Elmer. "And you remember what
I said, you just forget about that nonsense that
happened yesterday. Things like that happen to
us all the time. It's no big deal. You just have to
learn to forget about them."

Wendell nodded and started on his way home.
This time he knew he walked all the way. There
must be something I can do to help those horses
feel better about themselves, he thought. There
must be some sort of plan I can come up with!
But before he could come up with a plan,
Wendell had to come up with an idea.

"So?" Wendell's mother asked as he walked
into the apartment.

"So, what?" asked Wendell.

"So, how was the debate?" asked his mother.

"Oh." Wendell smiled. "It was great. I did
really well." Wendell didn't like lying, but . . .

"You see," said his mother. "You just had to
free yourself of all that worry, that's all. Now
what do you say . . ."

But Wendell wasn't listening anymore. Free
yourself, Wendell thought. Then he said, "I've
got stuff to do in my room, Mom." Wendell
Riley Randolph had just gotten an idea. A truly

stupendous idea. But it was going to need a plan. A very detailed plan. And help. He was definitely going to need help from someone. But who?

"*Wendell! Wendell!* There's a phone call for you! It's Judith Henderson. *Wendell!*" his mother was calling.

Judith Henderson! Of course! She didn't know it, but part of the idea was hers, anyway. Wendell Riley Randolph made sure his mother had hung up the extension, then, trying as hard as he could to control his enthusiasm, he began, "Judith — "

"Wendell, I'm hurt!" Yesterday you said we could go to the carousel today, and then today — "

"Judith, can you keep a secret?" he interrupted.

"Of course, I can, Wendell, but — "

"Are you interested in having an adventure?" Wendell continued.

Judith forgot how upset she was about the carousel. "With you?" she asked.

"It might be dangerous," Wendell added.

"What is it?" Judith had caught some of Wendell's excitement.

"And you can't tell anyone," Wendell said sternly. "Not anyone."

"Tell me!" Judith fairly screamed.

"Not on the phone, someone might hear,"

Wendell whispered. "I'll meet you tomorrow afternoon, right after school, in front of your locker."

Wendell Riley Randolph hung up the phone, took out his notebook and pen, and began to work out The Plan.

FOUR

"Come on, Judith, let's go to the park."

"But what about the adventure, Wendell?"
This had been the longest twenty-two hours and
thirty-seven minutes of Judith's life. Ever since
she had hung up the phone with Wendell, she
had been counting the minutes until she would
find out what he had been so secretive about.
She hadn't been able to concentrate on any of
her schoolwork. Twice in history class, which
was one of her favorite courses, Mrs. DuBrul
had called on her, and Judith Henderson, who
was always prepared with an answer (even when
she wasn't called on), hadn't even known what
the question was.

"I'll tell you when we get to the park," said
Wendell.

Well, Judith thought, I've waited this long. "Let's go."

As they approached the park, Wendell suddenly stopped. "Now, you swear to keep everything I tell you a secret? No matter what?"

"I swear."

"Even if you decide not to go along with the adventure?" Wendell continued.

"Yes," said Judith, solemnly.

"Swear?" asked Wendell.

"I swear," said Judith, who was beginning to get just a little annoyed, but was still able to hide it.

Wendell looked into Judith's eyes and knew she was telling the truth. "Okay. You see those horses over there? The ones that pull the carriages?"

"Yeah," answered Judith. "So?"

Wendell had known it wasn't going to be easy. But now, faced with actually having to say it out loud to someone whose opinion mattered to him, he was petrified. Wendell Riley Randolph, he said to himself, Just say it! So he did. "I talk to them," he said out loud.

"Oh, Wendell, you're just playing a joke on me!"

"No, I'm not, Judith. It's the truth."

"And I suppose they answer you, too!" Judith was getting angry.

"Yes, they do," said Wendell.

Judith wasn't just angry. She was furious. What kind of a joke do you think you're playing? she wanted to scream. I thought we were supposed to be friends! But Judith was so angry she couldn't even make the words come out. Which might have been a very good thing.

"I know it's hard to believe," Wendell was saying. "I know it sounds like I'm making it up. But I'm not. It's true. You just have to believe it."

Judith took a deep breath. In all the years she and Wendell had been friends, he had never been intentionally mean to her. He looked like he was telling the truth. He seemed desperate that she believe him. And why would he lie about something that would make him seem so silly? Maybe he was telling the truth. Maybe he talked to horses and maybe they talked to him. But that was impossible. Wasn't it?

"I do talk to them. And they talk to me," Wendell repeated.

There was something about the tone of Wendell's voice that made Judith start to think that maybe he was telling the truth.

"But how?" she asked.

Wendell took a deep breath. It was going to be all right. She was willing to listen. "It's a long story," he said. "Come on." And as they walked into the park, climbed a hill, and sat down on a big rock from which they could see the horses,

Wendell told Judith everything. About how he had learned to talk with horses from his uncle Chip. About Elmer and Old Barnaby and Winston and Molly and Archibald and Quentin and Angelina and Samantha and Cromwell and Chloe. About how overworked and how depressed they were. About what had happened the other day when that show-off police horse had made them all feel so bad.

"And so I want to do something special for them, Judith. I want to do something for them that's so wonderful, that for all the rest of their lives, any time they even start to get depressed, all they'll have to do is remember this thing and their sadness will just disappear. And they'll feel just as proud and special as any creature on Earth!"

"But what are you going to do?" asked Judith, nervously. She couldn't even imagine what sort of thing it was that Wendell had in mind.

"Do you promise not to tell anyone? No matter what?"

"I promise," Judith answered. And she meant it.

Wendell looked around to make sure no one was near. Then he looked Judith dead in the eye and very softly and sincerely said, "I'm going to set them free."

Judith didn't say anything for a long time. She couldn't. Her mind was racing with thoughts of horses running wildly through the streets of New York and of police dragging Wendell away to jail.

Wendell was still watching her when he quietly asked, "Will you help me?"

Suddenly the police in Judith's mind were dragging her off to jail as well. "I don't know, Wendell, I . . ."

"I got the idea partly from you."

"From me?"

"From what you told me about the carousel horses. About how at night they run free through the park," said Wendell.

"But that was pretend!" Judith was getting very scared. Wendell wasn't talking about playing a game. He was talking about *for real*! "I don't know, Wendell," she said, "I don't think we should do it."

"Look at them down there, Judith, knowing that for the rest of their lives they're going to be right there. Pulling those dumb carriages." Wendell was feeling stronger and stronger.

"I know," said Judith, "but it's illegal. Why don't we try to think of something else to do for them."

"This is it," said Wendell, firmly. "This is what I'm going to do. I know it's scary. I know it's illegal. And if you don't want to help, that's okay. But I'm still going to free those horses."

Judith looked at Wendell, then down at the

horses, then back at Wendell again. "They do look awfully unhappy," she said.

"They are awfully unhappy, Judith. They were humiliated. Cromwell told me that Elmer actually cried."

"But — " Judith began.

"And I don't mean we'd free them forever," Wendell continued. "Just for a couple of days. Just so they'd have something good to remember."

"But how will we do it?" Judith asked. "Where will we take them? What will happen to them? What will happen to *us*? What will people say?"

Wendell knew, even if Judith didn't realize it yet, that she had decided to help him. "We'll do it at night. Late at night, when everyone's asleep. We'll find a way to get into the stables where they're kept and we'll free them."

"How will we do that?" asked Judith.

"I'm not exactly sure yet," said Wendell. "I haven't worked out the details of that part of the plan. But once we do, I'll explain it all to Elmer, and he'll explain it to the others, so they'll all be ready. We'll take them way up to the north part of the park where it's wild and not many people go. And they'll be able to run and play all by themselves. But it will only be for two days. Two days. Then they have to go back. That'll be the deal. The night of the second day we take them back to the stables."

Judith wasn't so sure. "I don't know, Wendell. I mean, I'm not saying I'll do it, but if we do do it, I don't think that's such a good idea. I mean, it'll be too hard. If they've been missing for two days, there'll be all sorts of people looking for them. We'll get caught when we try to take them back."

"I didn't think of that," Wendell said, looking at his notebook.

"And if we got caught, we'd go to jail, Wendell." Judith's mind was once again filled with visions of she and Wendell, handcuffed, being dragged by the police into prison. Newspaper headlines. Her parents crying. Just bread and water to eat, and prison uniforms to wear. Everybody wearing the same thing. This was definitely not a good idea.

". . . Then we'll just have to find a better way. But that's why I need you to help!" Wendell was talking. Judith hadn't heard what he said at first, she was too caught up in her own thoughts about prison, but she had heard this last part — "That's why I need you." Maybe they could do it. Together.

"I know it's scary, Judith. I know it's dangerous. And I know we could get into big trouble. But it's important. And sometimes you have to be willing to take a risk, if it's for something that's really important," Wendell continued.

"What if," Judith began, very slowly, "what if,

the morning of the third day, they all just re-appeared."

"What?" asked Wendell.

Judith couldn't believe she was saying what she was saying, but somehow the words just kept coming out. "What if the morning of the third day they all just re-appeared? Standing right where they always stand, but without their carriages. As if they were saying to the world, 'We're here because we choose to be.' That would be easy to do. They'd just have to come down through the park and out onto Central Park South!"

"That's fabulous, Judith!" The words shot out of Wendell. "And Elmer told me he knows every inch of the park!" Wendell exclaimed. "So, he could lead them out! And we wouldn't even have to be with them!"

"But we could be there in the morning to see it!" Judith said. "It will be incredible to see all the people's faces!"

"Then, it's a deal?" asked Wendell.

Suddenly, Judith stopped. She took a deep breath. And then another. She swallowed. And then, very quietly, her voice shaking a bit, she said, "It's a deal."

They shook hands and swore a secret oath. They were going to spit in their hands and mix it together, but then decided that that was a "baby thing" to do, and that they trusted each other without it. The only thing left to decide was when.

"We're definitely going to need some planning time," said Judith. "Because we still don't know *how* we're going to free them in the first place. We'll need to look at the stables for that."

"I know," answered Wendell, "but I want it to be soon."

"So do I," said Judith.

What neither of them said, but both of them thought, was: *Because the sooner it is, the less time there'll be to get nervous.*

Wendell had taken a calendar out of his backpack. "How about . . ."

"May first," said Judith, pointing to the spot. "Friday, May first." The calendar said it was "May Day," whatever that was.

"Friday, May first," they both said in unison. "*May Day!*"

"Well," said Judith, looking nervously toward Central Park South, where the horses were standing, "shouldn't we go over so you can introduce us?"

Wendell thought for a second before answering. "I think we should wait until tomorrow. I haven't even told them about the idea yet. And I think I should do that first."

Judith was secretly glad that she was going to have to wait a day to actually meet them. She wasn't exactly sure what to say to a horse.

FIVE

The next morning, Wendell left home to go to school a little earlier than usual. On the way, he stopped to see Elmer and told him the idea.

"Now, we haven't worked out all the details yet, but that's the basic plan." Wendell could feel the smile on his face. "It's just for two days, that's all, but for those two days, you'll all be free. I'd like to see what that snooty police horse will have to say about that."

"I don't think he'll have very much to say at all," whinnied Elmer. "Now, what about this Judith Henderson? Can she be trusted? When do we get to meet her?"

"Of course she can be trusted," said Wendell. He was secretly a little hurt that Elmer would even think he'd involve somebody in The Plan who wasn't completely trustworthy. But, then again, he figured, Elmer was probably a little nervous, too. "This afternoon. I'll bring her by to meet you all this afternoon."

Elmer nodded his approval.

"Now, Elmer," Wendell continued, "you've got to promise me that you'll tell all the other horses. 'Cause it's got to be everyone. Promise?"

"I promise," said Elmer.

But then, Wendell was so excited, he told each of the others himself.

"Splendid! Splendid!" snorted Cromwell.

"We'll be able to hold our heads up again," sighed Archibald.

"You're such a darling," said Angelina, as she nuzzled Wendell's ear.

Quentin sounded a slightly negative note by saying, "It sounds like a wonderful adventure story. And you know how much I like you, Wendell, but you're still just a little boy."

"I'm twelve," Wendell reminded him. "I was twelve on the twelfth." Wendell felt a little hurt.

Winston thought it was a terrific idea. "And, even if it doesn't happen," he said, "just knowing that someone cares about us enough to try to do something so special, well, that's made me feel better already! And, Wendell," he added, "don't let what Quentin said bother you. That's just his way."

"Oh, I know that," said Wendell. But he was glad Winston had reminded him.

Chloe just giggled, which she did an awful lot, and Samantha said that it made her feel like she was back in the circus. (Though Wendell wasn't exactly sure why.)

Wendell even told Old Barnaby, who just stared blankly at the ground. Wendell Riley Randolph was worried about Old Barnaby. What if he got confused on May Day? Or wouldn't go? Or got lost? Or . . .? But Elmer told him not to worry, that he and the others would look after Old Barnaby.

"And," added Elmer, "two days in the park may be just what it takes to get those drugs out of his system and get him back to his old self. But Wendell," Elmer continued, "are you sure you can do this?"

"Sure, I'm sure!" exclaimed Wendell. (Though inside, he knew he wasn't only trying to convince Elmer, he was trying to convince himself, too.) Elmer threw back his head and whinnied so loudly that his driver stopped talking to the woman driver who always wore a tuxedo and top hat, and walked over to see if anything was wrong.

"He just likes being petted, sir," Wendell said sheepishly.

"Well, don't get him too excited, son," said the driver as he turned and walked back to the woman in the tuxedo.

"Okay, sir," Wendell called to the driver. Then Wendell winked at Elmer. "I've got to be going anyway. I'm going to be late for school. See you later."

After school, Wendell brought Judith Henderson to meet the horses.

"You're going to love them!"

She was very polite, saying "hello" and petting each of them on the nose. She had even brought her own sugar cubes and gave one to each of them. Wendell was right. Judith did like the horses. And the horses liked Judith. Each of them told Wendell so.

"Did you hear that, Judith?"

But try as she might, Judith couldn't hear the horses speak. So she just stood and watched.

"Don't worry, Judith, you'll hear them. It just takes practice. Why, it took me almost two weeks to hear Uncle Chip's horse, Simon. And over a week with Elmer. You'll see. You'll be able to speak with them."

Judith smiled appreciatively at Wendell. "Thank you for saying that," she said. "Are you sure?"

"Sure, I'm sure," answered Wendell. And he was. Uncle Chip could hear the horses. He could hear the horses. Judith would be able to, also. It just took time.

Judith, however, wasn't so sure. In fact, she was feeling pretty certain that this special ability that Wendell had — and that's what it was, she said to herself, a special, almost magical, ability — was not something that *anyone* could learn. It was probably something you were either born with or you weren't. It was like the way some people were just good at math. Judith was very good at math. It came naturally to her. Wendell wasn't very good at math, but Wendell could hear the horses. Judith was thinking that it didn't seem fair. She would much rather be able to hear the horses than be able to figure out some stupid math problem. But, though she was thinking all of this, she didn't say any of it out loud. All she did was keep smiling her appreciative smile.

"I think we should go and take a look at the stables, where the horses sleep," said Wendell suddenly. "We both need to see them. Even I've never been over there. And, like you said yesterday, we're going to need to know what they're like if we're going to come up with a plan of how to get the horses out of there."

"That's a good idea," said Judith. "Having them just come back by themselves at the end of the two days will be easy. But getting them free in the first place . . . that could be hard."

Wendell didn't want to hear about how hard it might be.

"We're going to have to plan that part very carefully," insisted Judith.

"I know," said Wendell.

Judith could feel herself smiling on the inside as well as on the outside. She might not be able to hear the horses, but Judith knew that she was very good at planning things. "Where are the stables?" she asked.

"West Forty-sixth Street," said Wendell, a little nervously. "Very West Forty-sixth Street. Almost to the river. Between Eleventh and Twelfth avenues."

The Hudson River was as west as you could go in Manhattan. It's what separates New York from New Jersey.

The smile vanished from Judith's face. Somehow, she had just assumed that the horses lived somewhere right by the park. West Forty-sixth Street between Eleventh and Twelfth avenues was quite a walk from the park. They were going to have to find a way to get the horses from Forty-sixth Street to Central Park without anybody seeing them. "Let's go have a look," said Judith, very seriously.

Wendell Riley Randolph and Judith Henderson began walking west to look at the stables. It was not an area either of them could remember having been in before.

"It's not a very nice neighborhood, is it?" said Judith, looking around.

Wendell didn't say anything.

"It's going to be pretty scary coming over here in the middle of the night to let the horses out," Judith continued. "And maybe a little dangerous, too."

Maybe more than a little dangerous, thought Wendell. But he didn't say it out loud. Out loud he said, "We'll just have to take a taxi."

"We won't be able to take a taxi!" Judith responded. "What we're doing — freeing the horses — is illegal. It's like stealing or kidnapping. Even if it is only for two days. Once those horses are gone and people start looking for them, a taxi driver is going to remember taking two kids to the stables in the middle of the night."

She has a point, thought Wendell.

"The same with the bus," Judith continued. "A bus driver would remember two kids going to this neighborhood late at night. Nobody *lives* here. There are just businesses and factories. Judith took a deep breath. "Which means we're going to have to walk."

Wendell didn't say anything, but he knew she was right.

The two continued walking in silence, looking around. This is *not* a very nice neighborhood, Wendell thought, even in daylight. At night these streets would be deserted and could be dangerous. Yet there had to be a way. There had to. They were standing in front of the stables.

"Look at the locks on the doors!" said Judith. "You can't open those from the outside unless you've got the keys."

"We could break a window and climb in," Wendell said, looking around, "except there aren't any windows."

"This is a real problem, Wendell." Judith wasn't trying to be negative. She really wasn't. She was trying to figure out a foolproof plan. She was trying to make it all work.

"We'll just have to be inside before they lock the doors," Wendell announced, wishing he knew how that could happen. They were both sitting across the street on the curb with their heads in their hands.

"I've got it!" Judith jumped up and started to the door.

"Where are you going?" Wendell started across the street after her.

"I just want to check something. Stay over there." Judith turned the doorknob. Slowly she pushed the door open and started to walk inside the stable.

"What do you want?" growled the gruff-looking man in old jeans and a plaid flannel shirt who was suddenly standing right in front of her.

"You kids is always coming around bothering me!"

Judith reached into her pocket. "I just wanted to give the horses some sugar cubes."

"Do you see any horses in here?" the man growled. Judith carefully looked around. " 'Course you don't," he said, " 'cause they're all out working. And I'm in here working, only I can't work if I'm talkin' to kids all the time, so get outta here!"

Judith started to leave, then turned. "Excuse me, sir, but when do the horses come home?"

"After midnight," growled the man.

"Oh, that's too late for me," she said and continued out. Just at the door Judith stopped again. "Does someone stay here all night with them?"

"What for?" the man said, laughing. "To sing them to sleep? Nah, they come home and we go home."

"Thank you for your time, sir," she said and was gone.

As the door slammed shut Judith heard the man muttering, "Kids! Always the same thing!"

"Come on, Wendell!" she called, starting to run.

"Where? What?" Wendell, who had sat back down on the curb, jumped up and started running after Judith.

"We've got to go see the horses again! Come on!" she yelled.

Judith and Wendell hurried back to Central Park South.

"Just as I thought!" exclaimed Judith as she stood looking at Elmer's carriage.

"Just as you thought, what?" asked Wendell, but Judith was already talking to one of the drivers; the woman in the tuxedo, who had her strawberry-blonde hair in a ponytail sticking out from behind her old top hat.

"Does the same horse always get the same carriage?"

"Oh yes, and the same driver, too," the woman said.

"Now isn't that interesting," remarked Judith. "Come on, Wendell, let's go into the park."

Wendell Riley Randolph started to say something but Judith cut him off. "We can sit on that rock again."

Wendell hated when Judith took over like this. After all, it was his idea. Maybe he should never have included her at all. Maybe he shouldn't have included anyone. Maybe he should have done it all by himself. Maybe . . .

"I've got it, Wendell! I've got it all worked out!" She was reaching into her backpack. "Want an apple?" Judith always came prepared. Wendell took one as Judith continued. "Did you notice that there's a little space under the seats of Elmer's carriage?"

"Mmmm," Wendell's mouth was full.

"And that Elmer's carriage is the last carriage in line?" Judith added.

"But not always. When a carriage comes back from a ride it goes to the end of the line," Wendell said as he ate his apple, being glad that Judith didn't know everything. "That way, every horse gets a turn."

"Well then," Judith said, deliberately, "Elmer is going to have to make sure he's at the end that night. You explain it to him. I bet he'll find a way."

"Why?" asked Wendell, as he swallowed.

"I'll get to that," said Judith, confidently, "just listen."

Wendell was going to say something about how this was all his idea in the first place, but instead, he just took another bite of apple.

"Have you ever lied to your parents?" Judith asked.

"Sure," said Wendell, a little too quickly. "Lots of times."

"I don't mean little, baby lies. I mean big, serious ones," Judith said. "Because that's what we're going to have to do to make this work."

Wendell thought for a moment. He decided that before he answered, he wanted to ask Judith something. "Have you?"

"Not really," she answered.

"Neither have I," admitted Wendell. "But if it's the only way to free the horses, then I'm willing to."

"I agree," said Judith. "Though I wish we didn't have to."

"What's the plan?" Wendell asked. He wanted to stop all the talk about lying.

"Well," said Judith, "you tell your parents that you're sleeping over at my house and I'll tell mine that I'm sleeping at yours. But instead, we'll come here. We'll have to figure out something to do for a few hours. But then, around midnight, when they're getting ready to take the horses back to the stables, we'll sneak into Elmer's carriage and lie down under the seats. One of the other horses can do something to distract the drivers. As long as Elmer's the last carriage, there won't be anyone behind him to see us. Then, we just lie there and let them drive us right into the stables. We won't have to worry about getting to that deserted neighborhood or opening locks or anything. Once we're inside, we sneak out of the carriage and hide behind the big pile of hay I saw. It should be easy because there weren't very many lights in there. Then we just wait for the drivers and that man to lock up and leave. Once they do, we're free to open the doors from the inside and lead the horses out. What do you think?"

Wendell thought that he was awfully smart to have asked Judith to help him. And he thought it was an excellent plan. And he thought he could have come up with one just as good. But, since this one was all worked out, they might as well use it. Wendell thought all these things and more, but what he said was, "Not bad. Of course we'll have to be sure to wear dark clothes so that we're harder to see when we sneak in and out of the carriage."

It rained the next few days. The horses didn't leave the stable and Wendell couldn't speak to them.

"What if it keeps raining through the first?" he asked Judith.

"It will stop," she answered. "It's got to."

And on the twenty-ninth, it did. Wendell went and explained the plan to Elmer. Elmer thought it was very well thought out and that he would have no trouble making sure he was at the end of the line. He also knew exactly which horse should cause the distraction so that Wendell and Judith could sneak into the carriage. "Cromwell," Elmer said. "Cromwell is the horse for the job."

"This is such a wonderful gift you're giving us, Wendell. No one has ever done anything special for us before. Look at them all, look at how different they seem."

Wendell looked at the horses and saw it was true.

"We have something to look forward to. Something to think about. And we'll have something to remember. Something besides work. We all thank you, Wendell."

Wendell went home, called Judith, and told her what Elmer had said. "Just two days to go, Judith."

"Have you told your parents you're staying over at my house yet?" she asked.

"I'm going to tonight," Wendell answered, feeling a little nervous about it, "at dinner. How about you?"

"I'm going to tell mine tonight, too," said Judith.

"Then there'll be no turning back."

SIX

"It's not that we don't trust you, Wendell," his mother was saying as she cut her lamb chop, "it's just that unless you let us call Judith's parents to make sure that they're going to be home and that it's all right with them that you stay over, we can't give you permission to go."

"But, Mom! Dad!"

"I don't think we're being unreasonable son," added his father. "Now eat your dinner and then we'll call the Hendersons."

Wendell finished eating, excused himself, and bolted from the table.

"Hello, Judith? We've got trouble. Have you told your parents about sleeping over yet?"

"I was just about to, why?"

"Well, I told mine and they want to call yours to make sure it's all right before they say yes. What are we going to do? If they talk to each other it'll blow the whole thing."

"Could we tell your parents the truth, Wendell — about the horses? Would they let us go?"

Wendell wished he could have answered yes. It would have made everything so much easier. They could get on with the plan. But the truth was . . . "No way, Judith. How about yours?"

"I don't think so. I mean, they're pretty understanding about a lot of things, but it would be awfully hard to explain this to them, I mean, about talking to horses and all."

Wendell was getting more and more upset. All of their planning, all of their time, all of their work was going to have been for nothing. He wasn't going to be able to free the horses because he wasn't going to be able to free himself. The horses! How would he tell the horses?!

He was barely listening to Judith. All he could think of was how excited the horses had been and how sad they were going to be. Suddenly he heard Judith say, "Wendell, I've got an idea! It's risky, but I don't think we have a choice."

"What is it?" asked Wendell, not caring how risky it was.

"Well," Judith began, "what if you came over here? My parents go to bed between eleven and eleven-thirty every night. We could wait until they're asleep and then sneak out."

Wendell wanted it to be a good idea. He really did. But he had to be honest with Judith, and with himself.

"Wouldn't the doorman wonder where we were going? And wouldn't he say something to your parents?"

"But what other choice do we have?"

Wendell was feeling terrible. Everything seemed to be falling apart. If only he were older. Then he could just say to his parents, "I'm going out, don't wait up, I'll see you in the morning." But he wasn't older. He was twelve. He was twelve on the twelfth and his special year was not turning out to be very special. Then, just as he was feeling the worst he had ever felt, Wendell Riley Randolph remembered something. Something that turned his feelings upside down.

"May first, Judith! May first!" he screamed into the phone.

"What?" answered Judith, trying to stop her ear from ringing.

"May first! The All Night Dance-A-Thon to raise money for muscular dystrophy!" Wendell was still shouting.

"Wendell, you're a genius!" Judith was holding the receiver away from her ear. "A genius!"

It was so obvious, Wendell couldn't believe he hadn't thought of it before. There were posters all over the school urging everyone to sign up for the Dance-A-Thon. He even had a flyer and parent-consent form in one of his books explaining the whole event. It was kind of like the charity walkathons where you got people to pledge a certain amount of money for each mile you walked. Only it was a dance. Each couple was supposed to get people — friends, parents, relatives — to pledge how much money they would give for each hour the couple danced. The maximum was twelve hours. The Dance-A-Thon, which was only for students in at least the sixth grade, started at eight o'clock in the evening, May first, after which the school doors would be locked. There were teachers who would serve as judges and chaperones. And there would be cots set up in the cafeteria for kids who needed to sleep. But no one could leave the school until morning — for safety reasons. Neither Wendell's nor Judith's parents could object, nor would they want to stay at the school all night to watch. All Wendell and Judith had to do was pretend to go to the Dance-A-Thon, kill a few hours, then head over to Central Park South and follow their original plan! "And we'll sort of be doing charity work, too," said Wendell. "Just for a different charity."

"And it will give us an excuse to pack some food," Judith added, "because it's going to be a long night."

Wendell returned to the dining room, flyer and consent form in hand. "I just called Judith," he said apologetically, "and I guess I got it a little confused."

"Oh?" said his father.

"She wasn't inviting me to stay overnight at her apartment," Wendell continued. "She was asking me to stay overnight at school."

"What?" asked his mother.

Wendell handed his parents the flyer. "To be her partner for the Dance-A-Thon. To help raise money to fight muscular dystrophy," he explained. "It's all there on the flyer. And you have to sign the consent form, too."

Wendell's parents looked at the flyer. Then they looked at the consent form. Wendell Riley Randolph just looked at his parents. This seemed to be going on for hours when finally Wendell's mother looked up and said, "Why, Wendell, what a wonderful thing to want to do."

"We're very proud of you, son," added his father.

It was working.

"But are you sure you'll be all right, staying up so late and all?" His mother sounded nervous. "Maybe you should wait until next year."

Wendell was about to protest when his father said, "He's twelve years old. He isn't a baby anymore. Besides, there'll be teachers there to supervise. This is the sort of responsible behavior that should be encouraged. There you go, Wendell." He handed him the signed consent form. "And we pledge three dollars for every hour you and Judith dance."

Wendell smiled at his parents. His "thank you" was little more than a whisper. "I'm going to go call Judith and tell her you said yes." But why did his father have to use words like "responsible behavior"?

The big night came. Before leaving his room, Wendell went to the bookshelf, took down his copy of *The Tales of King Arthur*, opened it to page twelve, and removed the two crisp twenty-dollar bills he had hidden there. He had gotten the money for his birthday — one from each set of grandparents. Both had written the same thing on their cards. "Use this for something special." Well, this is certainly something special, he thought. Wendell folded the bills up and put them in his pocket.

"Wendell," his mother said, "is that what you're going to wear to the dance? A black turtleneck, black jeans, and your denim jacket?"

"Sure, Mom. That's what everyone wears. Judith will probably wear the same thing." His heart was pounding as he said good-bye to his parents. It was really going to happen!

Wendell met Judith at her apartment. "You see, Mom," Judith said as they turned to leave,

"I told you black was in. See you tomorrow."
And they were off. The adventure had begun.

The first stop was the local vegetable market.
"I know that the horses will be able to find things
growing wild to eat, but some bunches of carrots
will be a nice treat," said Wendell. When the
greengrocer asked what they were going to do
with all those carrots, however, Wendell just
shrugged and answered, "They're for my mom,"
as he and Judith shoved the bags into their
backpacks.

The next thing to do was to stop by Central
Park South to let Elmer and the other horses
know that everything was under control. Then
came the hard part, finding something to do for
the next several hours.

"I've got the perfect idea," said Judith on the
way to Central Park South, "there's a theater
right across from the horses, next to the Plaza
Hotel. We can go to the movies. And afterwards
there's Rumpelmayer's a few doors down. We
can get some ice cream and watch out the
window until they start to get the horses ready
to go home. Then we just cross the street and
sneak into the carriage."

Wendell was pretty impressed with Judith's
thinking. Especially the ice cream part — all
adventures should include some ice cream!

Wendell and Judith didn't spend very much
time with the horses. They didn't want to draw

too much attention to themselves. And, anyway, most of the horses were off giving rides.

"Not too long, now," Wendell whispered as they passed the ones that were there.

"Oh dear, oh dear, oh dear!" giggled Chloe. "It's all so exciting! So terribly exciting!"

"We'll see you around oh-twelve-hundred hours," snorted Cromwell. Wendell didn't know for sure, but he was pretty positive that oh-twelve-hundred hours was military time for twelve o'clock noon and that what Cromwell had meant was, twenty-four hundred hours, which was twelve o'clock midnight. Of course, Wendell didn't want to embarrass Cromwell, and he wasn't completely sure himself, so he just nodded and said, "That's right, around midnight."

"It's going to be something," said Winston. "It's going to be scary, but it's going to be something."

"I wish it were time already. This waiting is just terrible." Angelina sighed.

"I know," Wendell said, smiling.

Old Barnaby didn't say anything. He just stared blankly ahead, which worried Wendell. But Elmer said, "Don't worry. He'll be okay," and Wendell believed him.

Through all of this, Judith managed to smile and not appear bothered by the fact that she still couldn't hear anything the horses said —

no matter how hard she tried. "Come on, Wendell," she whispered, "we'd better get going before we start to look suspicious."

After patting Elmer's nose and quietly saying, "See you later," Wendell and Judith crossed the street.

"*Now and Forever*! That's a love story!" exclaimed Wendell when he saw what movie was playing. "I don't want to see a love story!"

"Oh, relax, Wendell. What difference does it make what we see as long as it's here and it gives us something to do for the next few hours."

Judith did have a point. And as it turned out, it really didn't matter what the movie was, because Wendell had a hard time paying attention to it. His thoughts kept shifting to Elmer and Winston and Molly and Archibald and Quentin and Angelina and Samantha and Cromwell and Chloe and Old Barnaby. And when it was over, try as he might, Wendell couldn't remember a single scene.

At Rumpelmayer's, an ice cream parlor on Central Park South, Wendell and Judith sat down at a table from which they could see the horses across the street. They put the two backpacks filled with carrots down on the floor next to them and opened the menu. Wendell and Judith looked at all the delicious-sounding desserts. All the ice cream with hot fudge and whipped cream and fruit and nuts and marshmallow and brownies and cookies, and then they looked at the prices. And remembering how much they had already spent on the carrots and the movie, Wendell decided on, "One scoop of vanilla ice cream, please." "And I'll have one scoop of chocolate," said Judith.

"It's pretty late for you two kids to be out by yourselves, isn't it?" asked the waitress.

"We're older than we look," said Wendell.

"We were at the movies," said Judith.

"Oh," said the waitress as she went to take another table's order.

"We could tell her we're meeting our parents here," said Wendell as soon as she left the table. "Or that we're all staying at the hotel next door."

"Just leave well enough alone," Judith answered. "She wasn't really interested. Don't say anything more unless she asks."

It was 11:30 PM when the waitress brought the ice cream to their table.

"Here you go," she said. She put the dishes and the bill on the table and walked away.

"Eat slowly," said Wendell staring at the single scoop of ice cream in his bowl. "Very slowly."

At 12:25 Judith almost jumped out of her chair. "They're getting ready to go!"

For the past hour, Wendell and Judith had been going over the plan so that everything would go smoothly. They stood up, paid the bill, left a tip, slipped on their backpacks, and quickly and calmly left the ice cream parlor.

Once outside, they walked a full block west before crossing the street to the horses' side. Then they walked east past all of the horses. Wendell winked at Elmer, who was at the end of the line, but they didn't stop (they didn't want to draw any attention to themselves). When they were just past Elmer's carriage, they turned and waited. Suddenly Cromwell began whinnying loudly and rearing up on his hind legs.

"Whoa! Cromwell! Whoa! What's the matter boy?" said the driver as he tried to calm him, but Cromwell wouldn't calm down.

Cromwell's driver yelled to Elmer's driver, "Hey, Tommy, give me a hand here." Tommy ran over to help.

"*Now!*" cried Wendell as he and Judith jumped into Elmer's carriage and tried to hide themselves on the floor under the bench-seat.

"Squeeze in!" whispered Wendell.

"I am squeezing!" whispered Judith. "There's no more room!"

The space under the seats had looked bigger than it was. Wendell and Judith could be seen. But there was no turning back now. Cromwell had calmed down. Tommy had returned and the carriage had started to move. It was late and it was dark and they were wearing black and they hoped no one would notice them.

Elmer pulled the carriage faster than he had ever pulled it before as they headed home to the stables. He was pulling so fast that Tommy, his driver, had to keep all his attention on where they were going and couldn't turn around even for a moment.

"You're in a mighty big rush tonight, aren't you, Elmer?" Tommy called out. "Must be something awfully special back at the stable to make you run this fast."

Yet as fast as they were going, it seemed to Wendell and Judith to be taking forever.

"Where are we, Wendell?"

"I'm not sure," he whispered, "but we must be close by now."

"Well, look!" whispered Judith.

Wendell very carefully turned his head and started to look up when the carriage suddenly came to a halt. Wendell jerked his head back. "I think we're there," he whispered. His heart was pounding so loudly, Wendell was sure that the entire city could hear it.

What Wendell and Judith heard, however, was the sound of Tommy jumping down from the driver's seat. Then they felt the carriage start to move again, slowly, as Tommy led Elmer inside. It was dark in the stable, just as Judith had said it would be. Wendell poked his head up. Tommy was unharnessing Elmer from the carriage.

"Get ready!" Wendell whispered to Judith.

Tommy began walking Elmer away from the carriage and toward the horses' stalls. Wendell squeezed Judith's hand. "Let's go!"

From their hiding spot behind the bales of hay, Wendell and Judith watched as Tommy and the other drivers brushed the horses and got them settled for the night. It was nice to see the drivers patting the horses on the nose and slipping them little snacks, but when they said, "See you tomorrow," Wendell and Judith smiled at each other and shook their heads.

Finally, the last driver left, locking the door behind him. Wendell and Judith waited a few moments to make sure none of them was coming back, then they walked over to the horses' stalls.

"Good evening," Wendell said. "I know that Elmer has explained our plan to you all, but I want to go over it again, all together, before we start." There were general snorts and sputters as the horses voiced their approval. (All except Old Barnaby who just stared blankly at them.)

"Don't you think you should introduce us to your friend?" asked Angelina when she caught Wendell's eye.

"Oh, yes, yes, of course," apologized Wendell.

"We have been introduced, dear," said Molly to Angelina, a little snidely.

"Not all of us," answered Angelina.

"I can't imagine why not," responded Molly.

"Perhaps, because some of us were out working when she came by, instead of just standing around!" Angelina sputtered.

"*Ladies!*" Elmer interceded. "Wendell, please continue."

"For those of you who haven't met her," said Wendell, "this is Judith Henderson. And if it wasn't for her, we wouldn't be here now. She's a very good planner."

Judith, who had been looking at an old calendar on the back wall of the stable, turned more than a little red as she said, "Thank you, Wendell," and proceeded to walk about the stalls saying hello to each horse, starting with Angelina.

"Now, there are two parts of the plan which are the most important," continued Wendell. "The first is getting from here to the park. Judith and I discussed having you go in ones and twos by different routes so as not to attract too much attention. But then we decided that horses wandering all over the neighborhood might make people wonder whether the door had been accidentally left open. So, we agreed that the best way was the simplest way. To just walk to the park as a group."

"If all ten of you are walking together," Judith added, "anyone who sees you will just think that's what's supposed to be. Because that's the way people think — if there's a big crowd, it must be right."

"That's the way humans are, all right," said Molly.

"Now, a horse would know better," added Winston.

"We certainly would," said Samantha.

The other horses began to agree and Wendell waited a moment before quieting them. "The second thing is that you've all got to promise that first thing Monday morning you'll be standing, as usual, across from the Plaza Hotel."

The horses stomped their feet, nodded their heads, and sputtered their agreement. All except Old Barnaby, who just stared. Wendell walked over to Old Barnaby and began scratching his nose. "And that you will make sure Old Barnaby's there, too." Again, the horses agreed.

"It will be a terrific joke, won't it" — Wendell raised his voice to be heard over the snorts and whinnies and sputters — "to see you all standing by yourselves along Central Park South. No carriages. No drivers. Just you. Waiting."

The horses whinnied loudly, and even Judith knew they were laughing.

When they had settled down again, Judith

took over, explaining that they had some carrots, but, "You'll be on your own for food." Then she turned to Wendell. "Did they understand me?"

"Sure they did." He smiled.

"I still can't tell." There was a touch of sadness in Judith's voice.

Just then, Cromwell sputtered. It was an enormous sputter. He sputtered so loudly and for so long, that both Wendell and Judith spun around to see what the problem was.

"Three cheers for Wendell!" shouted Cromwell, once he had their attention.

"And don't forget Judith!" exclaimed Angelina.

"I wasn't going to," responded Cromwell. "You just didn't give me a chance to finish!"

"Three cheers for Judith!" shouted Samantha.

"Two days of total freedom!" snorted Winston. "Just think of it!"

"Oh dear, oh dear, oh dear!" Chloe giggled.

"And carrots!" Archibald sputtered. "Two days of freedom and carrots!"

"Oh, yes, oh dear, oh, yes. Carrots!" Chloe said.

The stable was filled with assorted stomps, snorts, and whinnies as the other horses joined in expressing their approval.

"Excuse me." Quentin, who had been at the rear of his stall, suddenly came forward and stretched his head out toward the others. "Excuse me," Quentin said again. His dirty white coat, covered with little gray splotches took on an eerie look in the dim light. "Excuse me," Quentin repeated for the third time. "I know how excited everybody is and what a wonderful adventure this sounds like it could be. But are we sure that this is really such a good idea? Look at us all. None of us has ever been free. We've, all of us, always been taken care of — sometimes better than others, but always given a stall to sleep in and fresh hay. And what about food? Are we sure we'll find things to eat? A few bags of carrots won't last very long among the ten of us. And water. What about water?"

Judith didn't know exactly what Quentin was saying, but from the look on Wendell's face she knew it wasn't good. "What's going on?" she whispered, nervously.

"Two days could be a very long time with no food or water . . ." Quentin was continuing. The other horses were starting to look concerned. Wendell turned to Judith to explain what was happening, when suddenly the entire stable was silenced by the loudest whinny Wendell had ever heard. It was Elmer.

"Quentin brings up some very important points," Elmer began. Wendell was getting very nervous. "Food and water are issues that must be addressed. True, some bags of carrots will

not last very long. But what Quentin, and perhaps some of the rest of you, have forgotten is
that I used to give horseback rides all through
the park, and I know every square foot of it.
And," he continued, "I know a spot with plenty
of grass to graze on and fresh water to drink."

Wendell smiled. It was going to be all right.

"What's going on?" whispered Judith.

"Shh," said Wendell. "Just a minute," as he
listened to Elmer.

"Now, as for none of us having ever been free
. . . that's true," said Elmer. "But I thought
that's what the reason for these two days was
in the first place."

"Of course it is!" yelled Cromwell.

"Three cheers for Elmer!" cried Samantha.

"I'm not saying it won't be a little scary,"
Elmer said, trying to quiet the others. "And,
Quentin, you're absolutely right to bring up
anything that's making you nervous, now, before
we leave. But I just don't think those things are
going to be problems."

"You tell him!" snorted Archibald.

"What do you say, Quentin?" asked Elmer.
"Wendell and Judith have done an awful lot of
planning. And they've already done much scarier
things than we'll have to do."

"Well," said Quentin quietly, "I just wanted
to be sure there'd be food and water."

"Three cheers for Elmer!" whinnied Cromwell.

"Three cheers for Quentin!" answered Elmer.

"Three cheers for Wendell and Judith!" said Quentin.

"Three cheers for everyone!" sputtered Angelina.

It was decided that three o'clock would be the perfect time to start out. It was late enough that the streets should be empty, but still gave them plenty of time to get up to the park before the city began to wake up. As the horses quietly snacked on some hay, Judith pulled some peanut butter and banana sandwiches and juice out of her backpack. "I thought we might need a little snack," she explained.

Judith was always prepared, thought Wendell.

Neither of them spoke as they ate. It was a time for quiet. The only sounds in the stable were the horses chewing their hay and Wendell and Judith chewing their sandwiches.

It was one-thirty when Judith finished eating and reached into her backpack. Out came a little traveling alarm clock. As she set the alarm for three o'clock, she said, "I think we should take a little nap — we've still got a long night ahead of us."

Wendell agreed.

SEVEN

BEEP BEEP BEEP BEEP BEEP BEEP BEEP . . .

Wendell and Judith jumped up, turned off the alarm, slipped on their backpacks and made sure they hadn't left anything lying around that might give them away.

"Let's go!"

One by one they let the horses out of their stalls, starting with Elmer, and walked them to the front door. When they were all assembled, Wendell very carefully turned the lock and opened the door just enough to stick out his head.

"All clear! Now, be careful." They opened the door the rest of the way. "Come on!" And out they all went, closing the door behind them.

"Here we go," Wendell said to Judith. "Are you scared?"

"Just a little," said Judith, trying to sound confident. "How about you?"

"Just a little," said Wendell, glad that he wasn't the only one.

When they got to the corner Elmer suggested that it would be much faster if Wendell and Judith rode. "Because it's a long walk and humans walk much slower than horses." Wendell thought this was a grand idea (he had learned to horseback ride from his uncle Chip — though always with a saddle, never bareback before). But Judith had never ridden a horse at all, "except for the wooden ones on the carousel."

Angelina stepped forward and said to Wendell, "I would be honored to give Judith her first real horseback ride. And I promise to be extra careful to make it as comfortable and safe as I can. Just tell her to think of me as a big, old armchair!"

Wendell helped Judith up onto Angelina and then climbed up on Elmer himself.

"Wendell," Judith said, her voice shaking just a little, "do you promise to ride right next to me?"

"I promise."

And they were off. Up Twelfth Avenue they went, Wendell and Judith atop Elmer and

Angelina in front, Winston and Molly right behind them, then a threesome of Archibald and
Cromwell on either side of Old Barnaby (so he
wouldn't get confused), followed by Samantha
and Chloe, and finally, bringing up the rear, was
Quentin.

"This is sort of fun," said Judith (although
Angelina wished that Judith wouldn't hold onto
her neck quite so tightly).

The few cars that were out didn't pay any
attention to them — just as Judith had pre-
dicted — and before long they were making a
right turn onto Fifty-eighth Street, which eventu-
ally led to Columbus Circle where there was an
entrance into the park!

"How's everyone doing back there?" asked
Wendell, twisting around and looking back.

"Wendell! Be careful! Face forward! You're
going to fall off!" said Judith.

As they entered the park and turned onto one
of the trails heading north, Wendell could feel
how much Elmer wanted to break out into a run.
Wendell knew he was a good enough rider to
let him. But Wendell also knew that if Elmer
began running, so would all of the other horses.
And if Angelina started to run, Judith was sure
to get hurt. And, besides, there was no telling
what Old Barnaby might do. He could get confused and go off in another direction. In the
dark, they might never find him. So Wendell

leaned down on Elmer's neck and whispered in
his ear, "Soon. Soon you'll be able to run
as much as you want." Elmer understood. He
continued to walk north; past Sixty-sixth Street
and the carousel, past Seventy-second Street
and the boat pond, past Eighty-sixth Street and
the ballfields, past Ninety-sixth street and up
to where the park grows wild.

"It's awfully dark up here," whispered Judith.

"It certainly is," Wendell answered.

"Do you know where we're going?" asked
Judith.

"Not really," he said.

"Oh," said Judith very quietly.

"I don't think I've ever been up to this part
of the park before," she continued. "It's sort of
scary."

It sure is, thought Wendell, but what he said
was, "It's not that bad."

"Do you think we'll be safe?" asked Judith,
not sure if she wanted to know the answer.

"Of course," said Wendell bravely. "Nothing
bad's going to happen, but even if it did, we've
got ten big horses to protect us. They could
stampede and stomp any bad guys who tried to
bother us."

"I guess so," Judith said as she looked around
again.

Around   One-hundredth   Street   Wendell

leaned forward and whispered into Elmer's ear, "Okay, boy, it's up to you to find a good spot." Elmer gave a short sputter to say he understood, turned off the trail, and headed into the center of the park. The others followed in silence. The only sound was the *clip clop* of ten pairs of hooves.

"I'll be glad when we get there. Wherever 'there' is," whispered Judith. "Because I'm beginning to get a little sore. I mean, it's not Angelina's fault, she's being wonderfully careful, but horseback riding is rough on your legs, and on your seat."

Wendell knew what she meant. He remembered how sore he had been at Uncle Chip's after his first few rides (not to mention how he was starting to feel right then) and he was about to tell Judith about it when he realized that Elmer had stopped. They had arrived.

"We're here, Judith!" Wendell whispered as he slid off Elmer. "I'll give you a hand getting down." As Wendell helped her off Angelina, Judith forgot about her aches and pains.

It was still very dark (it was 4:42 by Judith's watch), but their eyes had gotten accustomed to it on the ride and, with the help of the moonlight, Wendell and Judith were just able to make out where they were.

"It's a beautiful spot, just perfect!" exclaimed Wendell as he hugged Elmer and patted him on the nose. "You did a wonderful job!"

"It's not like being in the city at all," said Judith, looking around. "It's like we've traveled very far off into the country."

And indeed it was. They were at the edge of an open field surrounded by woods. The grass, or whatever was growing, was quite tall and there were little bushes scattered about. To their right was the smallest trickle of a stream, enough to assure the horses of fresh drinking water.

Wendell watched as one by one the horses began to explore their temporary home. Elmer, followed by Winston and Samantha, started running about the field. Angelina dropped her head at the stream for a long, cool drink. Quentin and Cromwell were independently exploring the woods, while Chloe had found a nice patch of grass to munch on. Molly and Archibald were gently nudging and playing with a somewhat bewildered Old Barnaby.

Wendell stood, watching the horses. There they all were. Running and playing and eating and drinking and *free!* And, as he watched, Wendell became aware of the fact that there were tears in his eyes. He wiped them but the tears kept coming. It was a different kind of crying than Wendell had ever experienced. He wasn't sad. He didn't hurt. He felt good. He felt very good. He felt better than he could remember feeling in his whole life. But, still, he was crying.

Judith put her arm around him and said, "You did a beautiful thing, Wendell."

"No," Wendell shook his head, "*we* did a beautiful thing, Judith."

Wendell thought it was very kind of Judith not to mention his crying, but the truth was that Judith's eyes were so filled with her own tears that she didn't even notice Wendell's.

Just then, Elmer came trotting over. "Wendell," he said, "why don't you and Judith go sit by that big tree over there." He turned his head to his left. "That's a nice safe place where we can take turns watching over you. It's not that we expect any trouble, but the park can get dangerous, and it is very late."

"Okay," said Wendell, glad that Elmer had brought it up. Then, turning to Judith, he said, "Let's go sit by that big tree."

Judith looked around nervously.

"Don't worry," said Wendell, "the horses will protect us. Elmer just told me."

"Oh!" Judith smiled at Elmer. "Thank you. Come on," she said to Wendell.

They took off their backpacks and settled themselves against the big, old oak. Elmer motioned to Archibald who positioned himself a short distance from Wendell and Judith to take the first watch.

"I've got some more sandwiches and sodas," Judith said as she opened her pack. "And I guess we can take out all these carrots now, too." She dumped them out onto the ground as Wendell did the same with his. There was quite a pile of carrots. Judith handed Wendell a sandwich and a can of soda.

Wendell and Judith sat, enjoying their sandwiches and watching the horses.

Dawn began to break around five o'clock. With the sunlight, Wendell and Judith were able to see that the spot Elmer had chosen was every bit as beautiful as it had seemed in the dark, and every bit as secluded. The horses continued to explore and romp in their new-found freedom.

"They all look younger. Don't they look younger, Judith?" asked Wendell.

"Absolutely!" said Judith as she watched Quentin and Angelina race the length of the field.

At five-thirty, Wendell knew that it was time to start heading home. The city was beginning to wake up. Soon, joggers and bicyclists getting their morning exercise would fill the park.

"Elmer!" Wendell called, "Judith and I have to get going."

Elmer came trotting over to the tree.

"Now, Elmer," Judith said, looking him straight in the eye, "there's a bunch of carrots here for you all to share when you want a special snack."

"Thank you," Elmer replied.

"You're welcome," said Judith, "and we'll bring some more later."

"That's very nice," said Elmer, "but you don't need to come back today. You've had a very long day and you need to get some sleep."

Judith was just about to say that they could still try to come back in the late afternoon, when she realized something. Something that started as a tingling in her toes and raced its way all the way up her body until she started to scream, "*Wendell! Wendell!* I heard him! I heard Elmer! We were talking! I didn't even realize it at first, because it seemed so natural. But he talked to me and I heard him!"

Wendell was very happy for Judith. He knew what a special moment this was.

Elmer insisted on taking them back to Central Park South. "You're much too tired to walk and, besides, two youngsters shouldn't be wandering in the park by themselves at this hour."

"But what if somebody sees you on your way back?" said Wendell.

"Oh, don't you worry about me!" Elmer laughed. "Now, up on my back, the two of you, before it gets any later."

Judith and Wendell waved good-bye to the other horses as Elmer carried them south.

At Central Park South, Wendell and Judith slid off Elmer and said good-bye. Judith gave him a kiss on the nose. Wendell gave him a pat.

"Be careful!" they called out as Elmer headed back to the other horses. "And have fun!"

As Wendell and Judith walked out of the park, the city was beginning to come to life. The sun was shining. Joggers were starting their morning runs. People were out walking dogs. Wendell looked at his watch. Not quite six-thirty. The Dance-A-Thon didn't end until eight-thirty. That's when the school's doors would be un-locked and the kids would be allowed to leave. They had two hours to kill.

"We could go to a coffee shop and have some breakfast," suggested Judith. "That would do it."

"Great idea," replied Wendell. The night's adventure had left him very hungry. And so, after bacon and eggs and potatoes and toast and juice, Wendell walked Judith to her building, said "Call you later" and went home. He barely said hello to his parents, who were in the kitchen having breakfast. He went straight to his room, fell onto his bed, and slept.

EIGHT

The clock said 7:10 as Wendell opened his eyes. It was very dark in his room, (someone had closed all the blinds) and for a few moments Wendell wasn't sure if he was awake or asleep. Had it all been real or was it just a dream? Wendell wasn't even sure if it was 7:10 in the evening or 7:10 in the morning. And if it was morning, which morning was it? He was awfully confused.

"Well, hello!" said his mother as Wendell walked into the kitchen.

"So, Fred Astaire decided to wake up," added his father. "Just in time to have dinner and go to bed."

"What?" said Wendell, rubbing his eyes. "Who's Fred Astaire?"

"How was the dance, dear?" asked his mother. Behind her, the television was tuned to the news. "Did you have fun?"

"How big a check do we have to write?" added his father.

"What? Oh, it was nice. We danced ten hours."

"And we pledged three dollars for each hour" — his father had his checkbook out — "so that's thirty dollars made out to the Muscular Dystrophy Association. We're very proud of you, son."

Wendell didn't like lying to his parents. It didn't make him feel very good. In fact, it made him feel pretty awful, but what choice did he have? He truly wished that he could change the subject when he heard the television newscaster say . . .

"And now to today's biggest story . . . Where are the horses? Hansom cab drivers had a shock today when they arrived at the stables this morning. The horses were all missing. Police investigators, called to the scene, say they are baffled. They can't seem to find any clues as to who took the horses, where or why. There has been speculation that some animal rights activist group or individuals may be behind the disappearance. This was fueled by the discovery of large quantities of animal tranquilizers at the stables. The ASPCA, which monitors animal working conditions in the city, says that it will

conduct its own investigation into the possibility that the horses are being drugged. And if they find reason to believe it to be true, to insure that it is stopped. Turning to other news . . ."

". . . What do you think, Wendell?"

Wendell was suddenly, frighteningly aware that his father had been asking him something and that Wendell had been so caught up in the news story that he had no idea what the question was.

"What do I think about what?" he replied sheepishly.

"I think you're still asleep," said his mother, laughing.

"I guess so," answered Wendell, more than a little embarrassed.

"I said," his father began again, "that we are very proud of what you did last night — raising that money for muscular dystrophy — and to celebrate we would like to take you out after dinner. Maybe to Rumpelmayer's for ice cream. We haven't been there in a long time."

"Rumpelmayer's?" asked Wendell. All he could think of was, what if they had the same waitress that he and Judith had had. What if somebody, anybody, recognized him from the night before and said something?

"I don't think so, Dad. I mean, I think I'm just going to want to take it easy after dinner. But thanks anyway."

Wendell's parents looked at each other with one of their "I guess he's growing up" expressions.

"I'm going to go call Judith," Wendell added, as he left the room.

When Judith answered the phone, Wendell didn't even say hello. "Did you see the news!!" he exclaimed.

"And the papers!" cried Judith. "It's on the front page of all the newspapers!"

"Did you see the part about how the police found the drugs those people have been giving Old Barnaby?"

"Uh-huh. And that they're going to investigate."

"Yeah!"

"Wendell," said Judith. "I'm a little worried."

"What's to worry about?" Wendell said.

They're going to investigate," said Judith. "The police are going to investigate."

"Of course, they're going to investigate," said Wendell, "but they're not going to find anything."

"But how can you be sure?" Judith was suddenly concerned.

Wendell didn't like hearing the concern in Judith's voice. Judith didn't get concerned over nothing. Now Wendell was getting nervous.

"Oh, what am I talking about?" said Judith. "It's a good plan. There is absolutely no way we can get caught. They have no clues. No one saw us go anywhere near the stables. And the last people anyone would suspect are a couple of kids."

"Right," said Wendell. He might have said more, but his voice was starting to shake just a bit.

"I mean, we've finished the scary part," Judith said, feeling stronger. "What's the worst that could happen? If they found us in the park with the horses, we could say we were just riding our bikes and then there they were."

"Exactly," said Wendell.

"And first thing Monday morning, they'll be back on Central Park South, as if nothing had happened. And everyone will forget about any investigation." Judith said confidently.

They agreed to meet outside Judith's building first thing in the morning (with their bicycles) to go check on the horses.

Judith was feeling much better when she hung up the phone. But Wendell's mind was beginning to race. What if there was a clue? What if they had accidentally left something in the stable? No, he told himself, you're being silly. We checked the stable before we left. We were very careful. But it had been pretty dark in there, even with the light on.

Sunday was hazy and overcast, one of those

gray days when it might rain at any moment, and then again one of those days when it might not rain at all. It was not a day that would bring lots of people into the park for walks or picnics or ballgames or boat rides or anything else. That pleased Wendell. It pleased Wendell because even though he knew that the horses were safe and well-hidden and able to take care of themselves, he also knew that the fewer people there were wandering in the park, the less of a chance there was that someone might happen upon Elmer or Angelina or Cromwell or Chloe or Samantha or Quentin or Winston or Archibald or Molly or Old Barnaby. Wendell and Judith agreed to be as careful as possible, to take no unnecessary chances, to draw no attention to themselves.

First stop — carrots! Wendell and Judith bought two bunches each at six different green grocers, so they wouldn't cause anyone to ask, "What are you going to do with *all those carrots?*" Next, backpacks bulging, they took the most complicated route they could imagine to get to the park, to make sure no one could follow them. Then they criss-crossed the width of the park, doubled back, and only then turned off in the direction of the horses. It took a long time to get there. Several times they turned off the path, rode a while, and then circled back to the path. Finally they arrived at the spot where

Elmer had taken them the other night. *But the field was empty! Where were the horses?* Wendell looked at Judith. Judith looked at Wendell. All of the color drained from their faces. Their eyes glared wildly.

"*Where are they?*"

"*Elmer!*" cried Wendell, looking around.

"*Angelina!*" yelled Judith.

"*Where are you?*"

"Maybe we're at the wrong place," said Judith, hopefully. "I mean, neither of us really knows this part of the park, and it was dark when Elmer took us here. We must have made a mistake."

Wendell wanted to believe she was right. He wanted to believe it right down to his toes. But . . . "Look around, Judith. There's the little stream. There's the clump of bushes. There's the big, old oak tree we sat against."

"Maybe there's another spot just like this." There was panic in Judith's voice. "Maybe . . ."

"There is no other spot!" Wendell was shouting. "This is it! This is where we left them! This — "

Wendell jumped as he felt something tug at his backpack. He turned around. "*Elmer!*" And there they all were.

"How did you . . .?"

"Where were you . . .?"

"You see," said Elmer, "we can take care of

ourselves pretty well. We've been taking turns as lookouts. It was Cromwell who heard you coming." Cromwell sputtered proudly. "Of course we didn't know it was you then, so we hid. Not bad, huh?" Elmer nuzzled Wendell.

"Not bad at all," agreed Wendell as he scratched behind Elmer's ears.

"Good job, Cromwell," said Judith as she gave his nose a kiss.

"So, how are you all doing?" asked Wendell.

The horses responded with an assortment of whinnies, snorts, sputters, and hoof stomps. As Judith dumped the carrots out of the backpacks and went around giving one to each of the horses, Wendell told them all about the news reports. He had even brought copies of some of the newspapers and showed the horses the front pages, MISSING IN ACTION, HANSOM HORSES HIJACKED, and WHERE OH WHERE HAVE THE HORSES GONE?

"And the best part," Wendell proudly announced, "is that the police discovered the drugs they've been giving to Old Barnaby. And the ASPCA is starting its own investigation into it. And they've promised that it will be stopped and that the people responsible will be punished!"

There was another mighty chorus of whinnies and snorts and sputters and hoof-stomping.

"That's wonderful news, Wendell," said Elmer

when the horses had calmed down. "And now, we've got a surprise for the two of you. Someone we'd like you to meet."

Wendell and Judith looked at each other in a puzzled sort of way. What did Elmer mean? Who could he want them to meet?

On Elmer's signal, all the horses parted and there, standing alone in the middle of them, was Old Barnaby. His eyes were clear and alert. His feet were steady. His head was held high. He looked so young and healthy that Wendell and Judith almost didn't recognize him.

"Thank you," said Old Barnaby. "Thank you for giving us a weekend to look back on for the rest of our lives. We will never forget you. And hansom cab horses for generations to come will be told about the wonderful gift you gave to us, and in a way, to them."

While Old Barnaby was speaking, the horses had formed a circle around Wendell and Judith and were now loudly showing their agreement with Old Barnaby.

"Thank you," said Wendell.

"Yes, thank you all," added Judith.

"But we didn't do all this so that you would stand around and thank us," continued Wendell, "so go on and enjoy yourselves."

The horses didn't move. They stood looking at each other until Elmer stepped forward.

"Wendell," he began, "I'm about to ask you

for something on behalf of us all that I really
have no right to ask. We know that we made an
agreement and we will honor it, you have our
word on that. But we would like to ask you for
one more day. One more day of freedom."

Wendell and Judith looked at each other.
Elmer continued, "Yesterday was terrific and
today is wonderful. But tomorrow is Monday,
adults are at work, kids are at school. We could
really have the park to ourselves, really be free,
wander about a little more, be a little less
careful."

"I don't know . . ." Wendell started to say.

"And one more day would really be good for
Old Barnaby," Elmer added.

"Well . . ." said Wendell.

"And finally," continued Elmer, "that police
horse is off on Saturdays and Sundays, but
tomorrow he'll be walking his beat across Central Park South and he'll be sure to know about
us. But it's up to you, Wendell. We'll do whatever
you say."

Wendell didn't know what to say. On the one
hand, the plan had been for two days. They had
all agreed. But on the other hand, Elmer did
have a point about Old Barnaby and about the
police horse. But on the other hand again, what
if this was the start of a plan by the horses never
to go back? What if every day they asked for
one more day? Wendell knew that game. He

had often played it on his parents. But the horses wouldn't do that to him. But what if they did? Or what if they just refused to go back? Wendell couldn't very well force them. They were bigger and stronger than he and Judith. And there were ten of them. But they *would* go back. They were his friends. They just wanted one final day of freedom to last them the rest of their lives. Was that really asking all that much?

"Okay," said Wendell, "one more day. But you've got to promise that first thing Tuesday morning . . ."

"You have my word," answered Elmer. "You have all our words. Horses' oath."

Wendell smiled, even though inside he was a little nervous.

But when Judith said to him, "I'm not so sure this is a good idea, Wendell," he so earnestly convinced her, that he also convinced himself.

All the rest of the day laughter filled the area as Wendell and Judith played with the horses. In the afternoon, Elmer and Angelina gave them rides, and Wendell and Judith imagined they were pioneer settlers exploring new, uncharted territory. If any uneasiness had remained with either Wendell or Judith, by six o'clock, when they said their good-byes and pedaled home, it was long forgotten.

"Bye, Wendell," Judith said, as she was walking her bicycle into her building.

"See you in school tomorrow," he answered.

"Want to ride our bikes so we can . . ." Judith noticed the doorman, Joe, impatiently holding the door open for her. ". . . so we can go play explorers in the park again?"

"Sure," Wendell called as the doorman said, "Judy, are you coming in or staying out? I can't hold this door open forever."

Wendell rode off and as Judith walked into the building she turned to Joe and said, "My name is Judith. Never call me Judy. It's *Judith!*"

NINE

"It's Judith!" said Wendell's mother as she handed him the phone. "Tell her we're having dinner and you'll call her back later."

"Hi," said Wendell. "I can't talk now. We're eating dinner."

"*We have to talk now,*" answered Judith, her voice in total panic. "*It's an emergency!*"

"Wendell!" His mother was calling him back to the table.

"Just a minute, Mom!" Wendell's voice shrunk to a whisper. "Judith, I can't talk now. They won't let me. And they're right here in the kitchen. I'll call you back as soon as I can. I promise."

"Wendell, did you see the news? *They know!*"

"What does who know?"

"Wendell, I'm scared!"

"Wendell, hang up the phone *now!*" This time it was his father.

"I'll call you right back, Judith, I promise." Wendell hung up the phone. His mind was racing. What did she mean? What was going on?

"What did Judith want that was so important?" asked his mother as Wendell sat down.

"What? Oh, she has a big test coming up. In science. And she's sort of panicked about it. I told her I'd go over it with her." Wendell wolfed down the rest of his dinner and asked to be excused.

"What about dessert?" His mother sounded annoyed. "We've got apple pie and ice cream."

"I'm too full." Wendell knew his parents weren't happy. "Maybe later," he added, hoping to smooth things over a little.

His mother was exasperated. "Okay," she said, "go call Judith."

"Thanks!" Wendell bolted from the table and went off to use the other phone.

"So, what's going on?" asked Wendell when Judith answered.

"I was watching the news," began Judith, "and they were talking about how the police still didn't have any real clues about what happened to the horses but that they did have a new possible lead. And there he was!"

"There who was?" asked Wendell.

"The man from the stable!" said Judith. "The one I talked to that day. He was saying he didn't know if it meant anything, but a couple of days before the horses disappeared there had been this girl who came by the stable asking all sorts of questions about the horses. And he said he couldn't really describe her but that he thought she had brown hair and she was . . ." Judith paused a moment, then, very quietly continued, ". . . and she was overweight. And he was pretty positive that she wasn't one of the neighborhood kids."

"And that's all?" asked Wendell.

"That's me!" cried Judith.

"Judith, how many girls with brown hair do you think there are in New York who aren't from that neighborhood?" Wendell decided to ignore the part about "overweight." Judith wasn't overweight, she was just Judith.

"But what if one of the drivers . . . what if Elmer's driver remembers a brown-haired girl and a boy who spent a lot of time with the horses? What then?" asked Judith.

Wendell was starting to catch some of Judith's concern. "But that's perfectly logical," he said, trying not only to convince Judith but to convince himself as well. "We like the horses, we spend time with them, and we wanted to see where they live. Perfectly logical. It's just a silly coincidence that we went to the stables a couple of days before the horses disappeared. It's not like it was the same day."

"We should never have agreed to let them stay away an extra day," cried Judith. "They would have been back tomorrow morning and everyone would have forgotten about the girl with brown hair. But now there'll be another whole day for them to investigate!"

"First, you've got to calm down." Wendell was trying as hard as he could to sound relaxed.

"Calm down?! That's easy for you to say, Wendell Riley Randolph!" exclaimed Judith. "They're not talking on the news about a blond boy with glasses and a few freckles. They're talking about *me!*"

"But we're the only ones who know that," he began. "All they're talking about is a girl with brown hair."

"Today, maybe." Judith was not convinced. "But what about tomorrow? What if we left something somewhere? What if they find something? A clue."

Why did she have to say that? Why did she have to say, "What if we left something," Wendell thought, as he felt the beginnings of panic.

"We've got to do something, Wendell!" Judith exclaimed.

But what could they do? It was Sunday night. It was too late to go to the park and tell the horses they'd have to stick to the original plan and be back by tomorrow morning. Wendell's mind was racing. There must be something they could do. Something that would make the police forget about that girl with brown hair.

"I've got it!" cried Wendell. "This stableman's story isn't much to go on. It's just that it's all they've got. What if they got a stronger lead?"

"What do you mean?" asked Judith.

"I'm not really sure," Wendell admitted, his mind still racing. What did the earlier reports say? Were there other theories? Wait a minute! What was it Judith had said the other day? "What we're doing is illegal. It's like stealing or kidnapping." Of course!

Wendell wasn't even aware that Judith was in the middle of saying something when he exclaimed, "What if they got a ransom note?"

"What?" said Judith.

"A ransom note!" repeated Wendell. "A ransom note saying that the horses have been kidnapped. That would make them forget all about a couple of kids."

"But . . ." Judith began.

"Just leave it to me," Wendell said, reassuringly.

"But . . ."

"I'll meet you tomorrow morning in front of your building on my way to school," he continued.

"But . . ."

"We'll ride our bicycles, so we can go straight to the park and visit the horses right after school." He had the idea. He just needed to work out a few details. A ransom note. Kidnappers. It was perfect. And then, first thing Tuesday morning, the horses would be back and it would all be over.

"But . . ." Judith had begun again.

"Don't worry! Everything's going to be fine."

Judith hung up the phone and tried very hard to believe what Wendell had told her.

TEN

```
We  have  the  missing  horses.
We  will  contact  you  tomorrow
about  ransom.  Pay  or  they
will  be  turned  into  dog  food.
```

Wendell sat back and looked at the note he had typed. It seemed pretty good. Short, to the point, and (most important) it didn't seem like it was written by a kid. He thought the part about dog food was particularly clever. Wendell had seen a movie once where some old horses were sold to a dog food company. He remembered how upset everyone in the theater had been at that scene and thought it was just the sort of thing to ensure that the ransom note would get lots of news coverage. The only question that remained was, who to give it to. If there was more time he could mail it to the police or a newspaper. But that would take too long. It was Sunday night, it had to be delivered by the next morning. He couldn't just hand it to someone. Wendell sat staring at the note, not knowing what to do.

Actually, Wendell knew what he wanted to do. He wanted to call Judith. Judith would have an idea. Judith would be able to figure out the one little part that was missing from his plan. Judith was good at that. But Wendell also knew that as much as he wanted to, he couldn't call Judith. She wouldn't be very good at planning anything right now. The whole purpose of this plan, the whole purpose of the ransom note, was to calm Judith down by making everyone forget about the "girl with brown hair." But Judith wasn't going to calm down unless he could show her a perfectly worked out solution.

Think, Wendell, think, he kept telling himself. But all he could think was, call, Wendell, call.

"Call! Of course!" he actually said it out loud. It was so obvious. Why hadn't he thought of it before? They could call in the ransom note. Tomorrow morning from a pay phone on the way to school. But to whom? The police? No, too risky. The television station? The one that had interviewed the man from the stable. No, they might tape the call and play it on the air and then someone might recognize his voice. The newspaper! The one his father called "that awful rag." They'd print it! They'd print it on the front page!

Wait till Judith hears this, he thought. Those reports about a brown-haired girl who was asking about the horses are going to just disappear! I should call her now and tell her to relax.

"Wendell!" His mother had poked her head into his room. "What are you still doing up?" She was not happy. "Do you have any idea what time it is? It's Sunday night! You have school tomorrow! We thought you'd gone to sleep a long time ago."

"Yes, mom," Wendell replied. He would have to wait until he saw Judith in the morning to tell her the plan.

Wendell got into his pajamas, turned off the light, got into bed, and quietly started to practice disguising his voice — trying to make himself sound older. It was very important that he not sound like a kid when they made the call.

"It seems like a good plan," said Judith, when they met the next morning.

"Of course it's a good plan," said Wendell, wishing she had been a little more enthusiastic.

"But do you think it will work?" Judith asked.

"Of course, it will work!" answered Wendell. "Come on, let's go find a pay phone."

Wendell and Judith parked their bicycles up against the phone booth.

"First, we've got to call information for the number," said Wendell.

"I'll do it," said Judith, as she squeezed into the phone booth with him. "So it's not the same voice that calls the newspaper," she added.

Wendell thought that there was no way anybody could connect a phone call to information and a phone call to the newspaper. And besides, even if they could, they would never know who made them. But Wendell also thought that it was best not to bring it up. Maybe this was just Judith's way of saying, I want to be a part of this.

"555–6600. 555–6600," Judith repeated the number. "Got it?" she asked.

"Yeah," Wendell said, as the two of them squeezed past each other to switch places in the phone booth. "Ahem," Wendell cleared his throat. "City desk, please." He practiced making his voice sound deeper and older one more time before dialing.

"Wait a minute," said Judith as she began to search through her backpack.

"What?" asked Wendell as Judith's elbow accidentally hit him in the stomach.

"Sorry," said Judith without looking up. "Here it is!" Judith pulled the T-shirt from her gym uniform out of her backpack. "Cover the receiver with this when you talk. It will muffle your voice and make you sound older."

Wendell thought he was doing a pretty good job of disguising his voice and sounding older without the T-shirt. But all he said was, "Sure." He took the shirt, wrapped it over the receiver, dropped a quarter into the slot, and dialed. "555–6600." He turned to Judith, "It's ringing!" This was it.

"City desk, please," Wendell remembered seeing a movie on television where someone had called in a story to a newspaper and asked for the city desk.

"What did they say?" whispered Judith.

"One moment, please," Wendell whispered back.

"City desk," said a voice on the other end of the phone. Wendell took a deep breath. Here we go, he thought. "Listen, because I'm only gonna say this once. We have the missing horses. We'll contact you again tomorrow, same time, about ransom. If our demands aren't met, they'll be turned into dog food. Ya got that?"

Judith was squeezed right up against Wendell, trying to hear the response.

"Sure," said the voice on the other end. "But how do I know this is for real? How do I know you've really got them?"

Wendell covered the mouthpiece and looked at Judith. "He wants — "

"I heard," said Judith. "Tell him that against the back wall of the stable there's a really old calendar with a picture of some astronauts walking on the moon."

Wendell did. Then he added, "You can check it out, we'll call you tomorrow," and hung up the phone. "How did you know that?" he asked Judith.

"I saw it when you were talking to the horses. Did it work? Do you think he believed you?" asked Judith as the two of them tried to squeeze out of the phone booth at the same time.

"I think so," answered Wendell as he finally let Judith get out first.

By lunchtime all the newspapers had head-lines about the ransom demand. And the radio and television news reports were carrying the story, too. They were even starting to hint that it might have been an inside job done by someone who worked for the stables, since there was no evidence of anyone having broken in. The reports also said that the man who called about the ransom had tried very hard to disguise his voice and sound like a kid. But that it hadn't fooled the people at the newspaper.

The horses were a major topic of conversation at school that day. It seemed that every kid had his or her own theory about what had happened to them and whether or not they would ever be found. One boy, Gary Schwartz, (who everyone thought was weird) said that he had read that out west UFO aliens had beamed whole herds of cattle and other animals up into their spaceships to study them. And that he was absolutely sure that the same thing had happened to the horses. Someone else said that Gary Schwartz must know, because Gary Schwartz was a UFO alien, and everyone laughed. All day, Wendell and Judith just stayed out of the discussions and smiled.

After school, Wendell and Judith rode their bicycles to the park. They said hello to all of the horses, gave them each some sugar cubes as a treat, and told them about all the news coverage that their adventure had gotten.

"But then, there I was," said Judith, "watching television with my parents, and who comes on the screen, but the man from the stables."

The horses began to mumble.

"Him!" snorted Molly. "I could tell you a few things about him. And none of them are particularly nice."

The other horses sputtered in agreement.

"Let Judith continue," said Cromwell.

"Go on, dear," Angelina said as she nuzzled Judith.

Judith scratched behind Angelina's ears. "Then on television, in front of millions of people, that man said there was an overweight girl with brown hair who had come by the stable a few days before, asking all sorts of questions about the horses!"

"Oh dear, oh dear, oh dear!" cried Chloe.

"The nerve!" sputtered Winston.

"You're not overweight." Angelina nuzzled Judith again, which made her smile.

"So what did you do?" asked Cromwell.

"Well, Wendell came up with a marvelous plan," said Judith. "Tell them, Wendell."

And Wendell did. He told them all about the phone call to the newspaper and about disguising his voice, "like this." Wendell began making his voice as deep as possible. "Listen, because I'm only gonna say this once."

"That was very brave," sputtered Archibald.

"It certainly was," added Quentin.

Wendell didn't mention the part about threatening to turn them into dog food. He thought it might be too upsetting. And he was a little embarrassed at the thought of telling the horses he could even think of something like that. But he did tell them about all the news coverage the ransom note was getting.

"And everyone's completely forgotten about the over — " Judith looked at Angelina and stopped herself. "About the girl with brown hair."

At that point, Elmer stepped forward. "Wendell, Judith," he began. "Once again, I just want to say thank you from all of us, for all you've done. And especially for trusting us and giving us this extra day. You could have gotten into a lot of trouble. We know that. And so we thank you."

The other horses murmured their agreement.

"But," Elmer added, "and I think I speak for us all, I hope that you two aren't going to start making a habit of doing things like this. It would spoil all of our wonderful memories of these three days if this became the start of you two lying and stealing."

"Don't worry about that!" said Wendell. "This was special."

"And once was enough!" agreed Judith.

"Good," smiled Elmer. "And don't worry. We promise, at dawn tomorrow morning we'll be standing on Central Park South, across from the Plaza Hotel."

"We promise," sputtered all the other horses.

Wendell and Judith didn't stay very long. Old Barnaby insisted on giving them each rides as his own personal thank you, which they happily accepted. But then Wendell said, "This is your last day here. Judith and I talked it over and we decided that you should have it just for yourselves, so we're going to go now. Besides, it's almost five o'clock, and we've got to get home anyway. But we'll still see you every day. We promise."

"And we'll bring you treats and things," added Judith.

The horses had gathered around the two of them. Wendell and Judith hugged and kissed each of them: Elmer and Angelina and Cromwell and Chloe and Winston and Quentin and Samantha and Molly and Archibald and Old Barnaby, then they got on their bicycles and rode off. Wendell was so busy thinking about the horses that he didn't see a large pothole until it was too late. He tried to swerve but his bicycle skidded and Wendell fell to the ground.

"Are you hurt?" asked Judith, rushing to him.

Wendell brushed himself off, shook his head and said, "The next time we see them they'll be harnessed to those carriages. Every time we see them for the rest of their lives they'll be harnessed to those carriages. It's not fair!"

"I know. But at least they'll have had these three days. That's something." Judith was holding Wendell's hands, facing him. We should be very proud."

The next thing Wendell knew he had kissed Judith and she had kissed him and he felt sort of nice.

Wendell barely slept that night. First thing Tuesday morning he was up, washed, dressed, and in the kitchen having breakfast. His mother came in, turned on the radio, and said, "You're certainly ready early this morning. It's not even seven-thirty. What's going on?"

"I promised Judith that we could study for her science test one last time." Wendell was glad that after today he wouldn't have to lie to his parents anymore.

"You've been spending an awful lot of time with Judith lately," said Wendell's mother as she poured herself a cup of coffee.

"Yeah. Sort of," replied Wendell as he heard the radio announcer say, *"Good morning. It's seven-thirty and here's what's happening in the news, today, Tuesday, May fifth . . ."*

"I guess you're really growing up, Wendell." His mother had sat down next to him.

"Well, I'm twelve," answered Wendell as he tried to listen to the radio.

"I know." His mother sighed. "Twelve on the twelfth."

". . . The big story locally is the return of the horses that pull the hansom cabs. Early this morning the horses, who had been missing for over three days, mysteriously appeared on Central Park South at their usual post opposite the Plaza Hotel. Yesterday morning there had been contact from a man claiming to have the horses, stating that he would notify authorities today of his ransom demand. Police insist that no further communication had happened and no ransom was paid. Speculation is that the horses some-

*how managed to break free from their captors
and instinctively found their way back to Central
Park South . . ."*

"Instinctively?" snorted Wendell.

"What?" asked his mother.

Wendell desperately wanted to tell his mother
the whole story, so that she would know how
smart those horses were, and just maybe so
that she would know how smart he was, too.
But instead he replied, "Oh, nothing."

"I don't know why anyone would want to
kidnap those old horses," said his mother.

Wendell just shrugged as the newscaster continued. *"The horses were led back to their stables
where ASPCA veterinarians are examining them.
Preliminary word is that they seem to have been
very well cared for and that they should be
back on the street with their carriages by this
afternoon. Meanwhile, ASPCA officials are continuing their investigation into the horse tranquilizers found in the stables and the possibility that
one or more of the horses was being drugged.
They say the police will be questioning the
stable employees, and they repeated their earlier
statement that much closer watch will be given
to the treatment of the horses. Turning to sports
. . ."*

"Well, I've got to go meet Judith," said
Wendell, jumping up from the table. "See you
later."

"See you later," called his mother as Wendell raced out the door.

Judith was waiting in front of her building when Wendell got there.

"They're back!" she exclaimed.

"I heard," said Wendell. "They're at the stables being examined."

"I know," said Judith. "The radio said they'd be out this afternoon. We'll have to wait until after school to visit them."

Tuesday, May fifth was, without a doubt, the longest day Wendell had ever spent in school. On and on it dragged as Wendell daydreamed about the horses. It was no easier on Judith who, once again, was so distracted in history class that she didn't even know what the question was when she was called on. The other kids giggled and Mrs. DuBrul asked Judith to stay after class to talk.

"I don't know what's been going on with you the last week or so, Judith, but I certainly hope that whatever it is it's going to stop," Mrs. DuBrul began. "You've always been one of my best students. Now if there's some sort of problem, something I should know about . . ."

"There is, I mean, there has been, I mean . . ." began Judith.

"Would you like to talk about it?" asked Mrs. DuBrul. "It might help."

"Oh, no. It's personal. But it's almost over. I

promise. I'll be much better tomorrow," Judith
sputtered.

"Okay, then." Mrs. DuBrul smiled. "If that's
true, if you really do get back to being the good
student you've always been, then we'll just
forget about this past week."

"Oh, thank you, Mrs. DuBrul. I will. You'll
see," said Judith and she raced off to her next
class.

At long last the bell rang. Wendell Riley Randolph and Judith Henderson were free! They
raced off toward Central Park South. And, as
they approached, there were the horses, standing in front of their carriages looking as good as
could be. There were a lot more people around
them than Wendell had ever seen before. And
as Wendell and Judith drew closer he realized
that they were all petting the horses and telling
them how glad they were to have them back.

"Sometimes you don't really appreciate the
little things that make life nicer in the city until
you don't have them for a while. Like just seeing
the horses pulling their carriages day after day,"
a woman was saying.

"Exactly," replied an older man. "You start to
take them for granted."

"Can we come pet the horses every day?" a
little boy asked his mother.

"I don't see why not," she answered. "In fact,
I think that's a very good idea."

Samantha and Quentin and Archibald and Molly were off giving rides, but Wendell and Judith did say hello to Cromwell and Winston and Chloe. They told Old Barnaby how pleased they were to see him looking so alert. Old Barnaby thanked them and said, "I owe it all to you."

Angelina nuzzled Judith and said, "You look very pretty today," which made Judith blush. "I hope you keep up with your horseback riding," Angelina added, "because with a little work, I think you could become quite good at it."

There was a group of people by Elmer's carriage listening spellbound as his driver, Tommy, captured their imaginations with *his* story of what had happened to the horses. Wendell and Judith inched closer.

". . . And so," continued Tommy in a hush, drawing the crowd close around him, "as near as we can figure it, the horsenappers took them to a deserted warehouse somewhere on the outskirts of the city. They were cold and hungry and afraid. They were threatened with being turned into dog food. And what did they do? What did these brave horses do? Why, they overpowered their guards and escaped into the night."

Wendell looked at Judith. Judith looked at Wendell. Then they both quickly turned away again as they felt themselves starting to laugh.

"They walked and walked and walked until they got to this spot," said Tommy, gesturing to where they now stood. "Here, where they knew they were safe and where they knew they would be found."

As the crowd "oooooed" and "ahhhhhed" Elmer winked at Wendell and Judith. Suddenly Judith nudged Wendell and said, "Look!"

The mounted policeman had ridden his horse over toward them. Tommy continued to speak. "Why these horses are heroes. Heroes! They did what no other horses in the city could have done. They freed themselves. After three days no one had a clue of how to save them. Even the police couldn't help them," said Tommy pointing to the policeman atop his horse.

Wendell and Judith watched as Elmer and the others stood proudly with their heads held high in the air. The police horse's head dropped lower and lower as he tried to urge his rider to leave.

"Hooray for the horses!" someone shouted and the crowd joined in cheering and applauding. No one even noticed the policeman ride his embarrassed horse away. They were all too busy petting Elmer and Angelina and Cromwell and Winston and Chloe and Old Barnaby. Wendell and Judith squeezed in long enough to slip Elmer a couple of cubes of sugar, pet his nose, and say, "See you tomorrow!"

Then they started to walk away, looking back and smiling at all the attention and love being given to the horses.

"What do you want to do now?" asked Judith.

Wendell thought for a moment. Suddenly he remembered something that Judith had told him before their adventure had ever started. He looked around, swallowed, smiled sheepishly, then took Judith's hand and said, "Let's go for a ride on the carousel."

About the Author

Michael Slade is a playwright whose work has been produced in New York, Los Angeles, and Edinburgh, Scotland. He has written the books to three family musicals: *A Little Moon Christmas*, *The Gift of Winter*, and *Hansel and Gretel*. This is his first children's novel.

Mr. Slade lives in New York City near Central Park, where he is able to visit the horses daily.